DILLON BURROUGHS
DANIEL DARLING
DAN KING

ACTIVIST FAITH

FROM HIM AND FOR HIM

BIBLEDUDE PRESS
read. pray. serve.

ISBN-13: 978-0692798683

Cover design by Fistbump Media, LLC

Some of the anecdotal illustrations in this book are true to life and are included with the permission of the persons involved. All other illustrations are composites of real situations, and any resemblance to people living or dead is coincidental.

For information about special discounts for bulk purchases, please contact Fistbump Media Special Sales at sales@fistbumpmedia.com.

The BibleDude Press authors can be available to speak at your live event. For more information or to book an event with this or another BibleDude Press author, contact us at speakers@fistbumpmedia.com.

"The challenges in our country and world are many. Daniel Darling, Dillon Burroughs, and Dan King provide thoughtful, biblically guided analyses of several of the most pressing issues of our day, challenging the church to let Scripture be our primary guide as we advocate for those who are vulnerable. Read this book, but don't stop there: Let it move you into prayerful action."

—MATTHEW SOERENS, U.S. church training specialist, World Relief; author of *Welcoming the Stranger: Justice, Compassion, and Truth in the Immigration Debate*

"The authors of *Activist Faith* challenge all who take their apprenticeship with Jesus seriously to closely connect what they profess on Sundays with how they live the life of true discipleship on Mondays. Combining an engaging blend of biblical principles, captivating stories, and practical ideas, the authors give a compelling picture of how the gospel speaks to some of the most challenging issues of our time. Taking this helpful book to heart will encourage you to be a more faithful presence in God's good but broken world."

—TOM NELSON, author of *Work Matters*

"*Activist Faith* is a compelling book that deals with complex global issues. It is filled with stories of hope and struggle, helping us wrestle with what it means to have a faith that cares deeply for those who suffer. This hope-filled collaborative work will help us all learn what it means to love our neighbor."

—CHRIS MARLOW, founder and CEO, Help One Now

"Evangelicals are rethinking their involvement in politics, so this is a hot topic. It's a discussion worth having, and Daniel Darling is at the cutting edge of the conversation."

—MATT K. LEWIS, senior contributor, *The Daily Caller*

"Authors Dillon Burroughs, Daniel Darling, and Dan King do a great job of luring much of the American Christian church to a conversation already taking place among far too few Christians. It is a discussion about 'elephant in the room' issues that usually reside with us for far too long without resolution. Read this book and take responsibility for these same such issues and their solutions as you encounter them in your town, church, and home."

—CHARLES J. POWELL, founder of Mercy Movement, Mercymovement.com

"This generation has more tools than ever before for living generously. *Activist Faith* explores the fundamental connection between the desire to engage in the world and the realities of what it will cost. More than anything else, it empowers you to do good work for the sake of the gospel."

—MIKE RUSCH, COO, PureCharity.com

"As Christians, we are called to make a positive impact on our world—to make it a better place. *Activist Faith* is one of those amazing resources that educate people on the issues and equip them to make a difference. A must-read!"

—JEN HATMAKER, author of *7: An Experimental Mutiny Against Excess*

"*Activist Faith* meets the need of our time, offering examples of Christians responding to the social concerns of our world in ways that make a genuine and significant difference. In a culture where criticism of Christianity is often the norm, these pages provide a fresh perspective of what God's people are doing to help those in their community and around the world."

—BRIAN AND HEATHER PUGH, actors; founders, Team Hollywood

CONTENTS

ACKNOWLEDGMENTS

Books are not solo projects but the fruit of many hands, most of them unseen. We are grateful for those whose support and effort made this dream possible. We thank our fine editor Meg Wallin, whose polishing helped us cut much fat without losing the spirit and intent of the work. We also thank the many faithful Christians we interviewed who work in faith-based organizations big and small. It is your love of Jesus that fuels the mission and inspires us to invite other Christians to experience the joy of service. Lastly, we thank our spouses and children for allowing the many necessary hours of writing and rewriting. From Dillon—thank you to my wife, Deborah, and my kids, Ben, Natalie, and Audrey, for all you do to bring joy to my life. From Daniel—thank you to my wife, Angela, and my kids, Grace, Daniel, Emma, and Lily. From Dan—thank you to my wife, Krista, and my kids, Samuel, Chloe, and Audrey.

THE OTHER SIDE OF JUSTICE

I (Daniel Darling) wasn't like most other boys my age. While they salivated over fast cars, bulging biceps, and hot girls, I was more interested in what was going on in the world. I raced my parents to the mailbox to pick up our weekly issue of *U.S. News & World Report*, and every Sunday I poured over *The Chicago Tribune*.

I found I had a love for news. I was forming opinions on matters of consequence. For required oral reports and debates, I researched current hot topics, including abortion, euthanasia, AIDS, and the death penalty. I scoured library microfilm and back issues of magazines to learn about Watergate, the war in Vietnam, and other important stories from recent history. My reading included biographies of Ronald Reagan and other conservative luminaries.

One of the highlights of my high school years was an internship with a conservative political activist. I had a front-row seat to state government. We interns navigated the back halls of the capitol in Springfield, Illinois, and sat in legislators' offices, listening as they wrestled with tough voting decisions.

In high school and into college, I began to consume political media (mostly from a conservative perspective), and along the way I developed a typical right-wing portfolio of opinions on every issue from tax policy to welfare reform to NAFTA to hating on Clinton (in good Christian love, of course!). I wasn't too interested in other views.

Meanwhile, I was building a career as a writer and editor for a large Christian organization.

My political tastes ran on a parallel track with a call to Christian ministry, and often the two conveniently mixed. Our church stood politically connected and active, with fresh opportunities to get involved in Republican campaigns readily available.

In 2005, I was asked to assist a friend in his campaign for Congress. I served as the volunteer liaison to the evangelical community, with premium access to power players in Illinois and Washington. This was heady stuff! I frequently met with top-tier political celebrities and logged long hours crafting strategy and recruiting new volunteers. I canvassed the evangelical churches in our district, building relationships with ministry leaders and working to win their support.

This experience was, in a way, the fulfillment of a childhood fantasy. There I was, helping to shape the future of our government. But this joy was soon replaced by the cold hard reality of big-league politics, and I quickly realized that even the good guys often sacrifice their integrity to get ahead.

My backstage pass to the political process and my growing relationships with evangelical leaders in our area awakened me to a profound truth few Christian conservatives care to admit: Politics is surprisingly ineffective in solving social ills.

As my interest in politics waned, my love for ministry grew. There wasn't a onetime flash of lightning or vision from heaven but rather a slow walk away from a focus on the temporal of elective politics to the eternal impact on human souls. In this season, God refreshed a hunger to move from politics to the pulpit and called me to serve as pastor of a local church.

Now serving in my current position as pastor of a small suburban church, I have realized something that escapes the news media, the conservative and liberal media reporting, and the attention of most active Christians. While many fix their gaze on the political scoreboard, the ideological food fights, and the twenty-four-hour news cycle, we forget that the real solutions are frequently found in our own communities of faith. Those hotly debated issues are often being met head-on by quiet acts of service, born out of hearts transformed by God's grace through the work of the church.

In 2008, I accepted the call to pastor a small church in the northern suburbs of Chicago. Though I've been there less than five years, I've already seen what the church can do to effect change. In Lake County, evangelicals enjoy incredible cooperation, working together to meet the social needs of our people, and I meet regularly with area pastors across a wide range of denominations. We rarely discuss politics. What we do discuss is the spiritual life of the county and the roughly 600,000 unchurched men, women, and children here who need to hear the gospel. We consider ways to meet pressing new social needs. With every unmet concern, a committed group of Christian activists answers the call.

What's happening in Lake County, Illinois, is remarkable but hardly unique. If you look around the world, the church of Christ is actively engaged in meeting needs. It's not because a government coerces them or a political party seeks to score victories; it's because there is a faith in Christ that motivates the redeemed to action.

Today, more than ever, evangelicals are rising to the occasion, casting aside tired political arguments and getting dirty in the business of changing the world.

SO WHY THE BOOK?

In 2010, I began having discussions with my writer friend Dillon Burroughs and the "Bible Dude," Dan King. We wondered if there were a way to both highlight *and* mobilize the work of the church in addressing the very issues that feed today's political activists. We feel that underneath the noise is a rising tide. The result is a movement: ActivistFaith.org and this book.

We all agreed that the Christian community doesn't need another tired memoir by young evangelicals hating on the church. Besides, we don't hate the church. We love it! I'm a pastor of an evangelical church. Dillon teaches at a conservative seminary in the South and writes on issues of faith and culture. And Dan King is a Christian blogger (at BibleDude.net) who has taken an active role serving in the church and teaching others to live out the gospel.

We're writing because we are excited about the important discussion taking place in the evangelical world: Where are the lines when it comes to faith, politics, and the gospel (and, yes, we do believe there are some lines)? It's a conversation that involves conflicting cross-currents. There is the traditional old guard who has valiantly fought the culture wars against "those liberals" who are trying to remove God from our world. Yet there is a growing resistance to this mindset, especially among younger evangelicals who feel that this aggressive posture and limited portfolio has damaged the reputation of the church (and, by association, Jesus Himself).

Second, there is the tension when it comes to the church's mission itself. Many evangelicals believe that Christians should be involved in Great Commission pursuits alone, sharing the faith and discipling new believers. Others take the opposite approach, considering the traditional orthodoxy of the gospel too simple and believing that meeting physical needs is more important than meeting spiritual ones.

The Activist Faith movement seeks to address these issues with a holistic approach. We feel the Great Commission is essential but doesn't replace or compete with social action. We resonate with Dr. Tim Keller's view shared in a recent interview with *Christianity Today*:

> There is a division between evangelicals. Some feel that doing justice is not what the church is supposed to be doing; on the other hand, there is an overreaction to that among many younger evangelicals who would say the job of the church is word and deed equally. I want people to remember that the impetus for helping people comes from the experience of grace.[1]

We are also not advocating a retreat from politics by evangelicals. History is littered with devastating consequences when a church abandons its voice in the culture. And we know of many remarkable Christians who toil with little appreciation in our local, state, and national governments. As Michael Gerson and Peter Wehner, authors of *City of Man*, say,

> At any given moment in a democracy, great issues of justice and morality are at stake. The idea that people of faith can take a sabbatical from politics to collect their thoughts and lick their wounds is a form of irresponsibility. It is, in fact, an idea that could only be embraced by comfortable Christians.[2]

The Activist Faith movement isn't a call of retreat; rather, it's a call to advance or to engage, but in a more winsome, effective way. We desire to help Christians think through social issues in a thoughtful, gospel-centric way—to move from the tired left-right, cable-news, talk-radio mindset and toward healthy involvement that brings solutions.

THE ISSUE MATRIX

In the book of James, we read the challenging words of a church leader to his congregation, reminding that a faith that fails to translate into action isn't a worthy faith at all. This is why we believe that the greatest agent of change in our world isn't in the power centers of Washington, D.C., or New York; it's in the hearts of ordinary believers transformed by the power of Christ.

Our desire in writing this book is to serve as both cheerleaders and coaches. We bring to light ministries that are engaging tough social issues regardless of which party is in office. We also operate as coaches, challenging Christians to get involved.

We chose twelve key issues. This is not an exhaustive or definitive list but one that reflects current arguments in our society. We share biblical and cultural contexts for involvement, anecdotes from Christians on the ground, and resources to help ordinary people make a difference. As you read, ask God to speak to you and give you a clear direction of how you can act on His behalf, sharing His love and mercy with the many hurting people around you.

In the end, our goal is to encourage every believer to become an activist in the movement, doing good deeds in our world so that those who see may give glory to our Father in heaven (see Matthew 5:16). To Him be the glory!

>> >> >>

Dan's Take: One of the best things about this movement in my mind is that it's for *everyone*. This isn't about a couple of "important" people making their voices heard and making things happen. It's about every single man and woman who sits in a church pew on Sunday mornings (and some who don't) doing something awesome in response to the amazing gift we've been given.

I was a little intimidated about taking on this project with guys like Daniel and Dillon. I'm the only guy on this team who's not fully seminary trained and in some major leadership role in ministry. I'm the epitome of the term *laity* in the church. But I've come to realize that this is the beauty of my role on this team. I represent the everyday activist, because that's exactly what I am.

Being an everyday activist doesn't mean you need to quit your job, sell all your possessions, and move to a Third World country to feed starving children. In fact, one might even argue that staying in your job while finding ways to influence the world around you might even give you greater opportunities to discuss your faith with coworkers.

Being an everyday activist simply means that you are taking advantage of the opportunities right in front of you and embracing what God is calling you to do—and doing it with the full devotion you'd give if you were serving Jesus Himself. Because in truth, you are! I see my role in this as being a support to you and providing you the information and tools you need to succeed in the work you do.

This Activist Faith thing is a movement that really excites me, and I mean it excites me down to the core of my being! The opportunity to show the love, grace, and compassion that's been given freely to me is an act of worship that seems equal to little else.

>> >> >>

Dillon's Take: Daniel's words reflect our united goal in these pages: to encourage Christians to live what they believe. We cannot do everything, but we can all do something.

Over the past several years of writing and teaching students in churches and universities across the nation, I've sensed the growing tension between current evangelical leaders and the emerging generation of Christians. Interestingly, the controversy often has little to do with theological beliefs but more often with the consequences of those beliefs.

You may disagree with some of our conclusions, but please do not miss our hearts. We seek to serve Christ, reflecting His love in every aspect of our lives, including the troubling social issues of our day, such as homelessness, education, and the environment. Sitting on the sidelines in our interconnected world is not a sufficient response. The love of Christ compels us to act. As He has transformed us, we seek to help transform the lives of others.

What makes the Activist Faith approach unique is that we admit we cannot create social change in our own power. Many well-meaning people end life frustrated with the results they failed to achieve in this life. But when we rely on the power of Christ within us, the hope of glory, any success that is reached is credited to Him. We also have an eternal perspective, knowing there is life beyond this life—eternal life for those who belong to Christ.

Two concepts stick with me as I seek to address the issues of our increasingly global society. First, apart from Christ, we can do nothing (see John 15:5). Yet the New Testament also teaches that all things are possible with God (see Matthew 19:26). When we rely on Him, He can provide results beyond what we could conceive. Our power comes from Him and for Him.

May we ultimately be known as those who serve as He served, giving His life for many.

CHAPTER 1

FREE THE SLAVES (AGAIN!)

THE ONGOING SCOURGE OF HUMAN TRAFFICKING

Dillon Burroughs

Injustice anywhere is a threat to justice everywhere.

— Martin Luther King Jr., *Letters to a Birmingham Jail*

It may come as a shock to you to read these words: *Slavery still exists.*

In fact, there has yet to be a day in the history of the United States that has been completely slave free. According to the estimates by today's experts, anywhere from ten to thirty million slaves exist in our world today.[1] Does this shock you? I was certainly shocked when I first discovered this ugly truth. I had known from news headlines that sex slavery takes place in Southeast Asia, where groups such as the International Justice Mission (IJM) have been working to end slavery once and for all. But I thought our planet was actually about to end slavery.

This is not the case. On the contrary, thirty million people are more than double the number of victims who were transported during the entire transatlantic slave trade. According to the nonprofit organization Free the Slaves, slavery happens in nearly every country of the world, and the U.S. and Europe are not immune. Research that Free the Slaves conducted with the University of California, Berkeley, found documented cases of slavery and human trafficking in more than ninety cities across the United States.[2] After drug dealing, human trafficking is tied with arms dealing as the second-largest criminal industry in the world, and it's the fastest-growing.

But what exactly is human trafficking? According to the U.S. Department of Health and Human Services, human trafficking is the current legal term used for modern slavery. Victims of human trafficking are young children, teenagers, men, and women, and victims of human trafficking are subjected to force, fraud, or coercion for the purpose of sexual exploitation or forced labor.[3]

TOO CLOSE TO HOME

Early in our research, I met with a friend in a café in the northwest suburbs of Atlanta to discuss human trafficking and showed him the online tool I had found at SlaveryMap.org. We tested it and found a case of forced slave labor at a restaurant he had eaten at, only minutes away. Yet most people in the café where we were sitting likely had no idea these crimes had taken place in their own community. Likewise, when I tracked sex trafficking victims' situations near my office, I realized there had been incidents within walking distance. In fact, in the past two years, my state has reported sex trafficking cases in 85 percent of its counties.[4] But what can be done? What is being done? How can I be part of the solution?

That's what this chapter is all about: helping you do something to reduce the number of slaves in this world. I'll begin with some of my own story about getting involved in this area of social justice and follow with ideas other individuals, ministries, and organizations are implementing to help "be the change," preventing, freeing, and caring for modern victims of slavery and human trafficking.

MY DISCOVERY OF HUMAN TRAFFICKING

In June 2009, I had the opportunity to visit Haiti for the second time.

During my trip, I discovered the restavek system within the nation, a cultural phenomenon in which children from poor families are given or sold to those financially capable of supporting them. The deal is supposed to include food and housing and promises education for the children, yet this rarely happens. Forced labor and often worse occurs to an estimated 200,000-plus adolescents in the nation.

That November, I had made arrangements to visit Houston and was able to set up a speaking engagement at the church of a pastor who had taken the same trip with me to Haiti. As my Houston tour neared, I had started working on another research project related to human trafficking in the U.S., a phenomenon I knew nothing about until researching the Haitian forced-child-labor situation. At first I thought the plight of child slavery in Haiti was unique to the developing world. Certainly there weren't too many places you could buy a child, were there?

To my shock, I unearthed the ugly truth that modern slavery takes place within America's own borders. Our government estimates that 14,500 to 17,500 people are trafficked into the U.S. each year for some form of forced labor or sexual exploitation, not including the victims already within our borders. Once I learned this, I felt compelled to help. I joined up with another friend of mine, Charles Powell, in the Atlanta area and began the hard work of investigating human trafficking in our country.

As I prepared for my Houston flight, Charles said I should see if there was anyone in that area I could interview on the issue of trafficking. After all, Texas is considered one of the top spots in the nation for human trafficking, with estimates that more than 20 percent of trafficking victims pass through its borders. He even tracked down an organization online for me to contact named Home of Hope Texas. I called the number that week before my flight and a guy named Mark answered. The conversation was one of those things you could call a God moment.

I said, "I'm speaking in Houston this Sunday and wanted to see if I could meet about your work to fight human trafficking."

He asked where I would be speaking, and I answered, "Humble First Assembly."

"That's my church," Mark replied.

"Your church?" Houston has a population of more than five million people and several thousand churches. The odds that I would speak at the church of the *one person* I would call in the entire city were extremely slim. We decided God wanted us to meet.

After having lunch with him, I rode in his SUV to twenty acres of land where Home of Hope Texas is developing an aftercare center. I would soon volunteer to join their board of directors and help encourage their work to care for trafficking victims.

A year later, the work I began with Charles led to the opportunity to support another aftercare center in the Southeast. A third location is in discussion this year. Within the next year, there may be more beds available for the long-term aftercare of trafficking victims than existed in the whole nation in 2009. This is clearly a work of God, of which I am humbled to play a small part.

As I transition to the next stage of helping equip believers to make a difference in the modern abolition movement, my efforts are beginning to focus on one critical question I believe God placed in my mind during a radio interview on the topic: What if every church in America had a ministry to stand against modern slavery? Our goal must be to stop it from happening again. The accounts are almost unbearable to mention. Before we can help, however, we must understand some core facts of the crime.

HOW CAN THIS HAPPEN?

There are a variety of tactics criminals use to trap victims into slavery, but usually it involves exploitation of one or more of the victim's vulnerabilities. This could include any variety of social or economic circumstances that may affect his or her ability to resist or escape from the trafficker's control.

One example of how such tragic activities can take place in our own nation comes from the leader and founder of Courtney's House, a model of aftercare of trafficking victims based in Washington, D.C. Tina Frundt shared her story of surviving the brutality of sex trafficking:

> I was 14 years old, and the way the pimp came at me was that at first I didn't even know he was a pimp. He came at me like a boyfriend. Yes, he was an older boyfriend but he cared about me. . . . Six months later, he told me "Let's run away together. We can have a beautiful house and family." And I did believe him, and we ran away, and then the story changed and I met the other girls that he had in his stable. And I had to go out every night and work the streets — the alternative was being gang-raped by a group of pimps while everyone watched.[5]

Unlike many destroyed by this horrific crime, Tina has responded by helping others in a similar situation. Our efforts to fight human trafficking are to help those who exist in the shadows. Ultimately, we wish to prevent Tina's plight from happening to anyone else.

Charles' investigation into American sex trafficking unearthed this ugly scene that offers a window into how an international female can be forced into trafficking. Here's what he shared:

> Somewhere in the southeastern United States a frightened young Asian woman we'll call Linn trembles with fear. Tonight for the first time she finds herself in a dimly lit room smelling of pine-scented disinfectant, stale rice and desperation. Faking a smile, Linn stands in a lineup among other women who are much like her, as a man she has never met selects which of them he will pay for sex. She is praying he will choose one of the other girls.
>
> Linn did not choose to be a prostitute; she was brought to the U.S. by a criminal organization that promised her a job working as a

> maid for a wealthy American family. Yet upon her arrival in the United States, she was raped, beaten and told she would have to work in a brothel to pay the bill for her travel expenses to America—a bill she will never cease paying. Linn is now a sex slave and the latest victim of worldwide human trafficking.[6]

This is not the exception; this is reality for far too many women, both in America and beyond. The situation is tragic, but it is not without hope for change.

FIGHTING BACK

You may not yet realize the importance of this time in history, but let me assure you that this age is one of the most strategic in the history of the Christian church. In five years, when a person asks, "Who is doing the most work to help free slaves in our world?" my goal is for the answer to be, "Christians." When Christians serve the "least of these," whether those in poverty or those in slavery, we see the words of Christ from Matthew 5:16 fulfilled: "Let your light shine before others, so that they may see your good works and give glory to your Father in heaven."

Now that I've informed you about human trafficking and attempted to motivate you to act to free slaves, I want to caution you about the "market" for those involved in anti-trafficking. You may view a television program or read something online that promises that you can free a slave for only X amount of dollars. Please disregard any such claim. There is no set amount required to free someone from slavery. Although a few organizations will actually "buy" the freedom of a slave as a last resort, this is not typical (in fact, it's actually illegal). Instead, look for organizations that not only claim to free slaves but also work to prevent slavery or provide aftercare services for those who have escaped a trafficking situation. Only through reputable and holistic efforts is the cycle of slavery truly broken.

Many, myself included, are working to implement social media such as Facebook, Twitter, and online petition sites to change the face of modern slavery. The U.S. 2011 Trafficking in Persons national report included an important insight for today's online anti-trafficking activists. The entire document is huge, but one section caught my attention because I was personally involved in the material mentioned. It reads,

> As shown in the recent events in the Middle East and North Africa, the growing reach of new and social media platforms has empowered grassroots activists with an unprecedented means to disseminate information and foster popular movements. For a movement such as the fight against modern slavery, which draws much of its strength from grassroots efforts, new media may emerge as powerful tools for identifying victims and bringing their traffickers to justice. Just as modern slavery crosses borders through migrant populations and globalized supply chains, new media can provide international tools for raising awareness, sharing best practices, and demanding government action.[7]

We're already seeing positive uses to fight slavery on websites such as Change.org, which launches petitions and shares news and information to draw attention to human trafficking issues. Whether through issue-specific media or far-reaching platforms such as Facebook and Twitter, concerned parties around the world can connect and share information with a speed and breadth of access unimaginable at the start of the anti-trafficking movement just a decade ago.

My friend Charles is a mastermind at creating public momentum against companies that facilitate sex trafficking ads, sore spots that drive much of the illicit industries for prostitution and sex trafficking. In a post he shared with me on the topic, he offered his recommended strategy to remove ads for illicit services that are used to promote potential human trafficking. He said,

> In your town, you might have spas or massage parlors that promise hours like 10 p.m. to 2 a.m. Perhaps they advertise the women who work there using their body measurements or tout their services as for men only. Maybe they promote the fact that every month or so they have a completely new female staff. If you didn't know already, these establishments are not legitimate day spas or massage establishments. They are fronts for exploitation. When you start to look around, you'll probably be surprised how many of these places there are in your town and how boldly they advertise.[8]

Here are his four steps for how to start where you live:

1. Start a petition asking any publication these nefarious operations use for advertising to cease publishing their ads. It's not a First Amendment issue; it's a human rights issue. Demand that they stop.
2. Protest against any billboard company that sells their advertising space for these illicit establishments.
3. Ask local real estate companies who lease commercial property throughout your city to sign a pledge not to lease property to such illicit businesses. Ask those who currently do so to seek to cancel the leases of these operations as soon as possible.
4. Obey the law in all your efforts and get started.[9]

A GROWING MOVEMENT

In 2011, I had the opportunity to connect with Noel Thomas, a young abolitionist from southern Florida who leads Redeem the Shadows, a group focused on ending human trafficking. Meeting at CNN headquarters in downtown Atlanta, our team brainstormed ways to widen the impact of his then-upcoming awareness event called "Redemption Day," which took place on 11/11/11. Across the country, thousands of activists held concerts, flash mobs, protests, and other activities to create an unprecedented awareness of the need to stand against modern slavery.

Around that same time, there was an important meeting with trafficking survivor Chong Kim. This Korean-American activist has courageously reported her story of two years of trafficking across multiple states in an organized trafficking ring several years ago. Her full interview is shared in a book I coauthored, *Not in My Town*. Since that time, a breakthrough has occurred. Chong's story was picked up by a Hollywood producer and turned into the motion picture *Eden*; it is planned for theatrical release in 2013. Though not a Christian film, the movie will highlight her story in a way that has already opened many doors for her to speak out on the topic, preventing many others from suffering the same fate.

Finally, it is important to mention an event that took place in January 2012 involving Louie Giglio's Passion Conference. In addition to speaking out on the topic of human trafficking at one of the largest Christian conferences for young adults in the nation, he challenged college students to give generously and sacrificially on behalf of trafficking victims. The forty thousand students donated $3.3 million! Furthermore, the movement soon released the song "27 Million," by Matt Redman, dedicated to ending the slavery of the estimated twenty-seven million trafficking victims in our world today.

HOW YOU CAN HELP

These stories of positive change are exciting to share, but I want to also offer some of the best practices being discovered by those working to fight modern slavery. I believe that many of these can be used or adapted in your context to do something about the situation starting today.

- **Buy fair-trade products.**[10] Though not mentioned in depth here, slavery worldwide taints many of our Americanpurchased products. We often do not know details, as only one part of one product is sometimes involved, but the fact remains that slavery is part of our economy in a multitude of ways. To prevent such unethical labor, an entire movement known as Fair Trade has developed. Simply put, Fair Trade products have a variety of stipulations that root out any slave labor, guaranteeing the product is 100 percent slave labor free.

One organization I specifically recommend is WorldCrafts. Their mission is to bring hope to impoverished people around the world. WorldCrafts is a nonprofit and a member of the Fair Trade Federation, partnering to build microenterprise businesses that provide sustainable income and hope for a better life. WorldCrafts imports handmade crafts made by artisans living on nearly every continent. Discover more at WorldCraftsVillage.com.

- **Buy survivor-made products.** Increasingly, trafficking survivor groups are banding together to create jobs in the development of survivor-made goods. A favorite example of ours can be found at MadebySurvivors.com.
- **Report suspicious activity.** One writer in the area of human trafficking has noted that about one in three rescues of human-trafficking victims in America came about because an ordinary, everyday person saw something and acted. In some cases, it was noticing someone who lived at a place of employment and could not leave. At other times, actions have been more direct, involving assistance to a person fleeing for help and providing a route of escape. Report any suspicious activity to your local authorities as well as the national human trafficking hotline at 1-888-3737-888, operating 24/7 in English and other languages.
- **Hold corporations accountable.** Ever wonder what your favorite brands are doing to make sure their products are slave

free? At ChainStoreReaction.com, there is a great tool available for sending preformatted letters to most major brands. A second site with a similar goal is available at Free2Work.org and allows users to view ratings of major brands by name or product type.

It "makes sense that we would be concerned by the ways in which slavery flows into our homes through the products we buy and the investments we make. Slaves harvest cocoa in the Ivory Coast, make charcoal used to produce steel in Brazil, weave carpets in India—the list goes on. These products reach our stores and our homes."[11] We must be careful to evaluate our purchases to make sure we are not complicit in the slave-labor chain.

- **Be a force of prevention.** It has been said that Benjamin Franklin coined the phrase "An ounce of prevention is worth a pound of cure." This statement may be even truer regarding the prevention of human trafficking. Some areas in which you can get involved include:

  - Providing services to runaways and homeless teenagers
  - Ministering to ethnic groups, including offering conversational English courses
  - Reaching out to young women who are in female juvenile detention centers or prisons
  - Becoming a journalist and writing to speak out against trafficking

- **Be creative.** Support the fight against trafficking through awareness at concerts, art galleries, and other events. This option may be especially well suited for families, students, and small groups.
- **Create or distribute awareness resources.** Wear clothing or sport bumper stickers and similar merchandise that lets

people know about human trafficking and how they can stand against it.

- **Host an anti-trafficking event.** Many speak across the nation on the issue of human trafficking and can be contacted for special events. However, it doesn't require a traveling speaker to host an event. A local nonprofit leader, law enforcement officer, or other expert could be what you need to inform and inspire your audience to act. You can combine your efforts with other national initiatives, such as the annual Stop Child Trafficking Now walk (SCTNow.org), to raise funds to stop modern slavery.
- **Sponsor a child.** In 2009, I began sponsoring Wood Nelly Tipha, then a six-year-old child in rural Haiti, through Compassion International. Compassion sponsors more than 64,000 children in Haiti. That is 64,000 children who will never be forced into child slavery. Wondering how to stop modern slavery worldwide? I don't have all the answers, but Wood is one child who will not be forced into the restavek system, and it will be because a person who loves Jesus decided to do something. An organization Dan King supports, Help One Now (HelpOneNow.org), also offers child sponsorship directly to children at high risk of child trafficking.
- **Donate.** Every cause needs funding to operate. Fighting modern slavery is no exception. You may not think you have a lot to offer, but every dollar makes a difference. Check out some of the organizations mentioned in this chapter or log on to MercyMovement.com. Mercy Movement exists to help equip individuals and churches to start anti-trafficking ministries where they live. If your church isn't already working in this area (and very few are at this point), the Mercy Movement is your opportunity to start.
- **Pray.** We dare not forget the power of prayer. Pray every day for the reduction of the number of those suffering the

abusive lifestyle of human trafficking. Whether a farm laborer, an immigrant woman forced into the sex trade, or a domestic servant unable to leave her location, it is often prayer that paves the way for God to work. If you have the opportunity to share prayer requests with a group or church, please highlight this issue along with our efforts. We are certainly aware this is both a human and spiritual struggle.

- **Partner with reputable organizations.** To date, the International Justice Mission has been the leader in international efforts to combat modern slavery. I would encourage you to log on to IJM.org and read all you can about their efforts and how you can help. Of course, they're not the only ones. *Not in My Town*, a book I coauthored with Charles Powell, includes a list of several other ministries working to fight trafficking both in the United States and beyond.

  If you are a student on a high school or college campus, there are organizations and clubs you can join to help fight human trafficking. See what your campus offers. If nothing exists, you can start a club through IJM, Mercy Movement, or a similar organization and start freeing people today.

Gandhi is known for saying, "Be the change you wish to see in this world." This is great advice, but an event I spoke at led to a slightly different slant on this oft-quoted phrase. At a church in my town, I shared with a group of college students about modern slavery and human trafficking in America. After my presentation, a friend of mine asked how it turned out. I told him, "The women were all ready to start aftercare centers for trafficking victims, and the guys were all ready to blow something up!"

The problem with addressing human trafficking is not getting people fired up about it; it's finding constructive ways to help. The same is often true of other areas where our faith applies. It's easier to express anger than to create positive change.

My challenge to you is this: Learn all you can. Discover what is causing the problem and the underlying factors involved. As you do, you'll find helpful, nonviolent ways to change the situation. Then act. Do something. The world is waiting for you to do as my friend Charles says: "Don't watch the news. Do something that makes the news." Or as Jesus said, "Go and do likewise."

THINK IT THROUGH

Take a few minutes to digest what you've learned and answer the following questions. If you're reading this as a group, talk through your thoughts together.

1. Were you aware of the extent to which slavery still exists? How does it make you feel to know that many people continue to live in bondage, even in the United States?
2. What is one thing you could personally do to help fight modern slavery?
3. In what ways could you involve your church, school, or workplace to join the movement to stand against human trafficking? Consider some of the ideas in this chapter and choose an option to consider as a first step.

HELPFUL TOOLS AND RESOURCES

For Research

- *Not in My Town,* by Dillon Burroughs and Charles Powell (New Hope Publishers, 2011)
- *Not for Sale: The Return of the Global Slave Trade—and How We Can Fight It,* by David Batstone (HarperOne, 2010)

- *The Slave Next Door*, by Kevin Bales and Ron Soodalter (University of California Press, 2010)
- MercyMovement.com/media, to take a look at human trafficking statistics

For Action

- Go to bibledude.net/activistfaith to join with others fighting against human trafficking.

CHAPTER 2

IMMIGRATION NATION

BORDER ISSUES IN THE REAL WORLD

Daniel Darling

> The Christian response to immigrant communities in the United States cannot be "You kids get off of my lawn" in Spanish.
>
> — Dr. Russell Moore, associate dean, Southern Baptist Theological Seminary

In January 2011, nineteen-year-old David Morales had a dream far different than most young men his age: He wanted to start the largest church in Utah. An impassioned follower of Christ, David was an active volunteer with Mission Urbana in Utah and enrolled in a Bible college in Louisiana. But this God-given desire to serve in the ministry ran up against a secret David carried with him his entire childhood.[1]

David Morales is an undocumented immigrant. Some would call him an "illegal." He is a resident of the United States not by his own choice but because his parents slipped across the border when David was nine years of age. His life presents an interesting dilemma. He was raised and educated in the United States. He speaks fluent English and is an American by every standard except one: his legal status.

David's dream came to a screeching halt when U.S. Immigration and Customs Enforcement officials stopped the greyhound bus taking him from Utah to Louisiana for Bible college. When officials inquired about his immigration status, David refused to lie. He admitted that he was undocumented. David was arrested and forced to spend seventeen days in detention. His case became a national news story, with celebrities, politicians, pastors, and others pleading his case. Thirteen thousand citizens signed a petition urging the federal government not to deport David back to Acapulco, Mexico.[2]

David endured a lengthy and uncertain trial during most of 2011. In February 2012, a Utah court essentially shut down David's case. He was the beneficiary of a new deportation policy issued by the Obama administration, authorizing immigration officials to use prosecutorial discretion, allowing undocumented children who are in good standing with the law to remain on U.S. soil.[3]

David Morales is just one of millions of undocumented immigrants who live in the United States. Many, like David, are here through no fault of their own, having arrived with their parents. Others are here because they purposefully entered the United States illegally.

Followers of Christ are divided on this complicated issue. For some, immigrants like David are the symbol of what's wrong with contemporary America. They lament the lack of border enforcement as a threat to a sovereign nation. For others, David's plight is a tragic example of decades of outdated and failed immigration policies. In their view, America no longer echoes the words of Lady Liberty, who beckons all those who "yearn to breathe free."

Politically, immigration will continue to be a hot potato. As followers of Jesus, what should our response be?

WEIGHING THE ISSUE BIBLICALLY

In 2010, the Pew Research Center found that only 7 percent of adults say their faith shapes their views on immigration.[4] This means that our views are largely shaped either by the surrounding culture or by media consumption. Bryant Wright, former president of the Southern Baptist Convention, challenged this tendency: "If you allow your authority to be a politician or a political ideology or talk radio or news media when it comes to any issue in life over the Word of God, you are outside the will of God."[5]

Before we can properly act on our beliefs when it comes to immigration, we first need to see how Scripture informs this complicated issue. Unlike some contemporary issues such as abortion, where there is a clear-cut biblical imperative, immigration finds a more nuanced view from Scripture. A careful student of the Word might employ three tenets of biblical theology to form a working worldview: the God-given sovereignty of a nation's laws, the duty of God's people to compassionately care for the immigrant, and the multicultural mandate fueled by the Great Commission.

A Nation and Its Laws

God's people have always wrestled with the question of their relationship to the state. Jesus was once approached by an unlikely coalition of political adversaries. The Pharisees were the conservatives, strongly opposing the encroaching power of Rome, while the Herodians were the statists, more accommodating of Caesar. They agreed on only one thing: the importance of stopping this increasingly powerful rogue rabbi from Nazareth. Each side feared Him, so they conspired with an entrapping question, the sort of cunning political skullduggery that still pays well today. Their query was about tax policy: Is it right for an observant Jew to pay taxes to Caesar?

They knew there was no good way for Jesus to answer this and save face. If He sided with the Pharisees and said no, He could be branded by Rome as a dangerous insurrectionist. If He answered yes, He lost all credibility with the orthodox Jew. It would make Him an accommodating sellout, another politician unwilling to lead a revolution.

In response, Jesus requested a coin. He held up the currency and asked a leading question: "Whose likeness is . . . this?"

"Caesar's," they replied.

"Therefore render to Caesar the things that are Caesar's, and to God the things that are God's" (Matthew 22:20-21, ESV).

Jesus' deft answer left both Pharisee and Herodian speechless. He threaded the political needle. But these words were not just a clever political sound bite; they form the basis of a proper biblical view of a citizen's relationship to his human government. Most of us understand Jesus' words as a mandate to pay our taxes, but there is more here: Jesus was drawing boundaries around the kingdom of God and the kingdom of man.

First, He established limits for the state. Contrary to the contemporary Roman belief, Caesar was not God. Caesar was appointed by God and was, himself, subject to a higher, heavenly authority. The state served a role but had no authority over basic human dignity. Man was created in God's image, not Caesar's. Man is not a cog in the wheel of the state; he is a divinely crafted soul shaped by a loving sovereign.

This view of a limited government is expressed throughout the New Testament. Consider Paul's words of advice to the young pastor Timothy. He wrote, "I urge that supplications, prayers, intercessions, and thanksgivings be made for all people, for kings and all who are in high positions, that we may lead a peaceful and quiet life, godly and dignified in every way" (1 Timothy 2:1-2, ESV).

Paul, like Jesus, created space between the state and the citizen. He affirmed the authority of kings and all in "high positions" but also affirmed the God-given right to a quiet and peaceable life. He described this relationship between Christians and the government in more detail in Romans 13:1-7 and was later affirmed by Peter's words on the subject (see 1 Peter 2:13-17).

In a sense, by ruling well, the state acknowledges it is not God. And a gospel-loving follower of Jesus should make a well-informed, sober, responsible citizen. He obeys the laws because he affirms the sovereignty of God in appointing the leaders who make the laws.

As Christians, we obey the laws of the land unless they clearly infringe on our God-ordained duties (see Acts 5:29).

God's People and the Immigrant

The second tenet of biblical theology that must influence the immigration conversation is the narrative of the immigrant. Over ninety-two times, the Hebrew word *ger* is employed in the Old Testament. This word is typically translated "sojourner, foreigner, alien." Some Bible teachers have suggested that perhaps the best translation might be "immigrant."[6]

In a way, every human born into this world enters as a refugee, cast out of Eden because of sin. This theme of the immigrant continues along the Bible's story line. When God created a nation from Abraham of Ur, He commanded this pagan rancher to leave his ancestral homeland and go, "not knowing where he was going" (Hebrews 11:8, ESV). By economic necessity and divine miracle, Abraham's progeny immigrated as aliens to the more prosperous Egypt, and later God moved this now sizeable population toward the Promised Land. More than two million refugees wandered the Sinai Desert for forty years before conquering Canaan. In the book of Ruth, we see Boaz's intentional and generous care for Naomi (his relative) and Ruth (a foreigner and immigrant to Israel). Then there is the story of Jesus, who at times was an immigrant, perhaps an illegal one. At the very least, He temporarily faced life as a refugee (see Matthew 2:7-15). In a spiritual sense, Jesus is the immigrant who traveled the greatest distance, leaving His home in heaven to come to earth and die on the cross as a sacrifice for man's sin (see 2 Corinthians 8:9; Philippians 2:5-8).

In the age of the church, God's people are considered aliens, temporary residents in the kingdom of man but whose allegiance is to the kingdom of God (see 1 Peter 2:11). Followers of Jesus work as agents of the crown, bringing healing to a broken world yet looking forward to that better city, built for us by God (see Hebrews 11:16).

God's people should feel a sort of kinship with immigrants. This is why the Scriptures are replete with ordinances on how we treat the aliens around us.

From Old Testament Law, we can discern the spirit in which God views immigrants. Israel was to treat the foreigner in her midst with equal dignity as a citizen (see Exodus 12:49), and throughout the Old Testament, immigrants are mentioned in the same oft-neglected class as the fatherless and widows (see Psalm 146:9; Jeremiah 7:6; Ezekiel 22:7; Zechariah 7:10; Malachi 3:5).

In the New Testament, Christians are called to love their neighbors (see Luke 10:27) and offer hospitality (see Romans 12:13; Hebrews 13:2; 1 Peter 4:9).

Perhaps the most vivid example of a Christlike approach is Jesus' treatment of the Samaritan woman at the well. He intentionally interacted with her, violating long-held social norms. Faithful and patriotic Jews didn't intentionally engage the Samaritan people, who were considered racially impure. In John 4, Jesus:

- Prioritized a meeting with her (see verse 7)
- Drank from her pitcher of water, ignoring the social taboo (see verses 7-9)
- Offered grace to cover her checkered past (see verses 16-20)
- Invited her into His kingdom by salvation (see verses 25-26)
- Rebuked the disciples for their prejudice and lack of evangelistic compassion (see verses 27-38)
- Commissioned her as a missionary to her own people (see verses 39-42)

Jesus set forth the model for Christian ministry as He loved and healed those who were rejected and defenseless: prostitutes, cripples, women, children. How we feel about the most vulnerable among us is a reflection of how we treat Jesus Himself (see Matthew 25:40).

A Great Commission Perspective

There is one more perspective that must shape the church's response to immigration. We are in the midst of a "Pentecost moment" in America, where people from almost every language, tribe, and tongue are settling in. The white Anglo-Saxon is fast becoming a minority.

I've had many conversations with Christian people who fear the changing racial dynamic of their own neighborhoods. At the grocery store, at PTA meetings, at church they are seeing people of different colors and ethnic origins.

For many this is a cause for concern. The America they once knew is slipping away, replaced by a homogenized society with people from varying cultures. But how should followers of Jesus respond? Should we worry that white Anglos will no longer be the majority, or should we consider this mass migration the work of a sovereign God, allowing us the opportunity to hear and receive the gospel and then spread it to the far corners of the earth? In a piece for *The Gospel Coalition*, Matthew Soerens and I wrote,

> Central to our mission is the call of Jesus to "make disciples of all nations" (Matthew 28:19). The arrival of immigrants into our communities has brought the nations to our doorsteps. This movement of people is not an accident: the God who made all people also "determined the times set for them and the exact places where they should live . . . so that men would seek him and perhaps reach out for him and find him" (Acts 17:26-27). While economic and sociological reasons drive people's desire to migrate, we believe God has sovereignly superintended this movement of people to America so that they might come into a saving relationship with Jesus Christ and follow him as disciples.[7]

Christians need not fear the increasing multiculturalism, the mixing of races in America. In a way, this is a slice of the kingdom, where the global aims of the gospel will finally be realized. Revelation 7 describes this scene: "I looked, and behold, a great multitude that no one could number, from every nation, from all tribes and peoples and languages, standing before the throne and before the Lamb, clothed in white robes, with palm branches in their hands" (verse 9, ESV). This future heavenly display of worship will be a fulfillment of Psalm 2:8, in which King David prophesied a day when all the nations of the world would be given to the Son of God as an inheritance. It's the realization of Daniel's vision of the future kingdom of Christ, where "all peoples, nations, and languages should serve him" (Daniel 7:14, ESV). In this age of the church, we are experiencing a partial fulfillment of Daniel's vision, inaugurated at Pentecost and continuing today (see Acts 17:26-27).

THE COLLISION OF LAW AND COMPASSION

So how are Jesus' followers to reconcile the affirmation of a nation's rule of law and the duty to love the immigrant? And how should this shape our attitudes toward the twelve to fifteen million undocumented immigrants who reside within the borders of the United States? I think we need to consider the following eight important statements.

1. We must affirm the rule of law with grace.

John described Jesus as the epitome of grace and truth (see John 1:14). Jesus perfectly fulfilled the requirements of Old Testament Law yet was the embodiment of grace.

Christians must not simply look at the issue of immigration as a purely legal one. Yes, illegal immigrants have come here by breaking the law. This cannot be encouraged or rewarded. Yet must we reach for perhaps the highest penalty—deportation—in order to punish their misdeeds? Consider our laughable relationship to speeding limits. Most people view the posted sign as a suggestion, especially when navigating the nation's freeways. When pulled over for a citation, we are often indignant and try to plead out of the penalty. Then, when it comes to facing the consequences, we always choose the path to amnesty, such as attending traffic school, so we avoid the blot on our record and the corresponding insurance rate increase. But imagine if, suddenly, the governor of a state decided to "take care of this problem of speeding drivers" and passed more stringent, crippling penalties. Perhaps ten miles over might now result in a confiscation of a license or the impoundment of a vehicle. The protests from ordinary citizens would be profound.

You can't directly correlate traffic safety to the complicated issue of immigration, but we should approach the infractions of others—those who illegally entered the country—with the same compassion and mercy we hope to experience ourselves. If our only response to illegal immigration is "But they broke the law!" then we'd be hypocritical not to apply that same pejorative standard to ourselves when we commit what we think is an innocuous infraction.

2. We must acknowledge that for many who cross the border illegally, the decision is a difficult one.

Consider, for a moment, the Christian husband or father in Mexico. He's living in absolute economic despair, and there is no hope or future in Mexico. His children are starving, his pregnant wife is malnourished, and there are no charities to help them sustain life. He reads in his Bible Paul's words to Timothy about a man who doesn't provide for his family: "worse than an unbeliever" (1 Timothy 5:8). His heart sinks. But he also reads 1 Peter 2:13-17, which tells him to "accept the authority of every human institution." Like Rahab, who lied to protect the Jewish spies (see Joshua 2:3-5), he is forced to make a difficult choice between two competing biblical commands. Some in this situation choose to obey the laws of the land they wish to go to: America. Others choose to obey God's command to protect and provide for their family. But isolated in our comfortable American homes, we know nothing of the agony faced by refugees every single day.

I find it simply amazing that some American evangelicals have unlimited reservoirs of compassion for refugees and orphans from impoverished overseas countries yet lack that same grace for the children of the poverty-stricken families on our southern border. I appreciate these wise words of Jim Daly, president of Focus on the Family:

> The Christian community has got to find the right footing to be able to express truth and express those things that are lawful, and at the same time express the heart of God. I just don't think the heart of God is against somebody trying to do better. People need to abide by laws. But we don't want to dehumanize people or stigmatize people simply because they're trying to better their lives and help their own families. We've got to be careful that we do not do that as a Christian community.[8]

3. We must discourage and oppose the exploitation of illegal human capital.

What fuels much illegal immigration is the exploitation (by American businesses) of the undocumented status of many refugees. They pay them wages far below the prevailing wage. Followers of Christ should not only refuse to practice such modern-day slavery but also oppose it vocally. Scripture firmly prohibits this practice (see Isaiah 3:15; Amos 4:1; James 5:4). Richard Land, president of the Southern Baptist Convention's Ethics and Religious Liberty Commission, says that America has two signs at the border: one that says, "Keep Out," and another that says, "Help Wanted." It is an undeniable fact that many American companies operate using the below-wage, secretive handshake system to employ undocumented workers from Mexico. Scripture is clear that an employer who refuses to pay his workers a fair wage is in sin against God (see Luke 10:7; 1 Timothy 5:18), and followers of Christ should resist exploiting the precarious status of undocumented workers to pad their profit margins.

4. Our views on immigration must be shaped by Scripture and not contemporary political movements.

Both left and right have used immigration, like other issues, as a weapon in the quest for power. Much of the rhetoric in this debate is dehumanizing to the immigrant and antithetical to the gospel story. Furthermore, it's important that Christians do not cherry-pick one or two passages to support their side of the issue. Instead, they should consider a more balanced view of the tensions between law and grace.

5. We can simultaneously advocate for change in immigration law, compassion for existing undocumented immigrants, and tougher border security.

The media loves to boil all sensitive, delicate issues into "either/or" battles. Political campaigns seize on any nuance and force division where it might not exist. But as a follower of Christ, you can affirm America's need to secure its southern border *and* advocate for a long-term solution for existing undocumented immigrants *and* pray for needed overhaul for our arcane immigration policies.

6. We need to admit that the topic of immigration is both sensitive and divisive.

As with all other hot-button political issues, Christians should avoid championing simplistic slogans as solutions to the very complicated problem of immigration. This is a multilayered social issue that has no easy answers. Good people of faith will disagree on the mechanics of sound policy, yet we must agree to disagree charitably.

7. We must regard all immigrants, legal or illegal, as dignified bearers of God's image.

The people within our borders, regardless of how they got here, are not just masses or people groups. Each is a dignified human being, created in God's image and bearing His likeness. He is a soul for whom Christ died, a person worthy of Christ's salvation. Many are our fellow brothers and sisters in the Lord, who deserve the love and support of Christ's body. Dr. Russell Moore—associate dean of Southern Baptist Theological Seminary in Louisville, Kentucky—wrote in a widely distributed column,

> Immigration isn't just an issue. It's an opportunity to see that, as important as the United States of America is, there will be a day when the United States of America will no longer exist. And on that day, the sons and daughters of God will stand before the throne of a former undocumented immigrant. Some of them are migrant workers and hotel maids now. They will be kings and queens then. They are our brothers and sisters forever.[9]

A person's immigration status shouldn't relegate them to a lower class.

8. Our primary focus should be on serving the immigrants within our midst.

While political battles rage in Washington and key places negotiate policy, people of faith must continue to look for ways to serve immigrants locally and ease their transition into America.

HOW YOU CAN HELP

Given that we've outlined the scriptural focus on immigration, what can followers of Christ do to both shape the public debate and minister to the immigrants in our midst? There are really three avenues where Christians can effect change:

- **Shape the public debate.** Followers of Christ have an opportunity to speak both prophetically to the culture and in an edifying way to the church. Unfortunately, myths, fear, nativism, and political considerations often shape the immigration debate.

  Most of the negative perceptions of immigrants arise from incorrect information, myths that have bubbled up from the culture. This is a golden opportunity for influential voices to speak clearly and winsomely.

When it comes to the immigrant community, there is much misinformation regarding the economic burden and the motivations of those who come here to seek a better life. A responsible Christian obeys the Scriptures and seeks the truth (see Philippians 4:8) before spreading or believing facts that may not be true. Part of loving our new neighbors is believing the best about them (see 1 Corinthians 13:7). We can shape the public discourse by gracefully rebutting false arguments (see Colossians 4:6). To get started, I encourage you to visit the immigration section at ActivistFaith.org and read "5 Myths About Undocumented Immigrants."

- **Advocate systemic change.** Evangelicals have an opportunity to speak with grace and courage to our government leaders. Pastors, lay leaders, small-group leaders, stay-at-home moms, and active church members all know firsthand the difficulty of this issue because we have friends, neighbors, and colaborers who are caught in the net of a broken system.

  As I write this book, there is great momentum for immigration reform. Christian leaders from across a large swath of evangelical denominations have come together to form the Evangelical Immigration Table (EvangelicalImmigrationTable.com). They are encouraging ordinary citizens to sign the Evangelical Statement of Principles for Immigration Reform. You might sign this and perhaps let your local congressman and senators know that you are standing with immigrants. As with any political advocacy, it's best to be Christlike in your attitude toward those who disagree and to express your views in a way that respects those God has placed in authority.
- **Support local ministry among immigrants.** There are several ways to demonstrate the love of Christ to immigrants in your local community. I recently interviewed J. Lance Conklin, director of immigrant legal services for the

evangelical refugee organization World Relief. He shared the following ministry opportunities:[10]

- *Welcome immigrants to your church, regardless of legal status.* Most legal experts agree that ministry to immigrants should not be influenced by immigration laws. And churches should be willing to extend their ministry, regardless of someone's legal status. As Rick Warren has said, "A Good Samaritan doesn't stop and ask the injured person, 'Are you legal or illegal?'"[11]
- *Establish an immigrant legal services ministry.* Both documented and undocumented immigrants are often in need of legal services. Churches can help fill this void in one of two ways. Larger churches with staff resources can actually establish a legal services organization recognized by the government. World Relief offers counseling and guidance in getting such a ministry set up. Smaller churches, which may not have the budget for such a ministry, can simply point to available immigrant legal services in their local community. Conklin said, "Sometimes it's as simple as guiding an immigrant to the right services, helping with paperwork, or it can be as important as serving as their legal representative. At times, there may be no legal recourse available, but your presence and support offer great encouragement to the immigrant."[12]
- *Serve immigrants in detention.* More than 400,000 immigrants are detained, indefinitely, awaiting deportation or an immigration trial.[13] Conklin said, "Many of these are the breadwinners in their families and they worry about how to care for their children. Usually, social services helps the children, but you have situations with families being split up. There is a real opportunity for churches to help alleviate

some family suffering here and engage in prison-type ministry with evangelism and counseling."[14]

- *Provide basic adjustment help.* Churches can also help immigrants, whether undocumented or legal, adjust to life in twenty-first-century America. This is best done by networking with local social service agencies, anti-poverty organizations, and other local ministries. It may be as simple as providing guidance on meeting basic needs, welcome baskets, or even car rides to banks, libraries, and the post office. There are also opportunities for churches to "adopt" refugees from war-torn places around the world. Conklin said, "World Relief and other organizations help place displaced refugees into the United States. When they arrive, we ensure they have their basic needs met, but it is helpful for churches to perhaps take them in, help them adjust from their war-torn situation to modern life, provide a sort of family atmosphere."[15]
- *Teach ESL classes.* Many churches provide ESL (English as a Second Language) classes. This is both a genuine opportunity to build relationships that can lead to gospel witness and a way of loving your local immigrant community. Matthew Soerens said, "There is a great need for English language instruction, whether through large-group classes or one-on-one tutoring; almost all immigrants *want* to learn English, but learning a new language, especially as an adult, takes a lot of effort, and options for affordable classes are very limited in some parts of the U.S."[16]
- *Partner with an immigrant church.* Churches may choose to form fruitful partnerships with immigrant churches for mutual ministry and as doorways to ministry among immigrants and diverse people groups.

If God has placed the issue of immigration on your heart, I suggest you prayerfully consider where you might get involved. Perhaps you have the influence to lead a group from your church, campus, or neighborhood. Or maybe you and your family can contribute on your own. It may be as simple as inviting an immigrant to your home for dinner. According to the Billy Graham Center, only one in ten immigrants will ever be invited to an American home.[17] You as a member of Christ's local body have an opportunity to display Christ's love and open the door to sharing the gospel with a family God has sovereignly placed in your community.

THINK IT THROUGH

Take a few minutes to digest what you've learned and answer the following questions. If you're reading this as a group, talk through your thoughts together.

1. How do you reconcile the Bible's seemingly two competing ideas: the rule of law and compassion for immigrants?
2. What attitudes have you had or noticed in your social circles that may not square with your calling as a Christian to minister to immigrants?
3. How can you help influence the public debate on immigration?
4. What is one thing you can reasonably do to get involved in showing Christ's love to immigrants in your community?

HELPFUL TOOLS AND RESOURCES

For Research

- *Welcoming the Stranger*, by Matthew Soerens and Jenny Hwang (InterVarsity, 2009)

- *Christians at the Border*, by M. Daniel Carroll R. (Baker Academic, 2008)
- The Gospel Coalition blog entry "The Gospel and Immigration," by Matthew Soerens and Daniel Darling (http://thegospelcoalition.org/blogs/tgc/2012/05/01/the-gospel-and-immigration)
- "On Immigration and the Gospel," Southern Baptist Convention Resolutions (sbc.net/resolutions/amResolution.asp?ID=1213) (June 2011)
- Evangelical Statement of Principles for Immigration Reform (EvangelicalImmigrationTable.com)

For Action

- G92.org is a website (a ministry of World Relief) that shares information and opportunities to minister to immigrants in your local context.
- WelcomingtheStranger.com (also a ministry of World Relief) offers a free "Learning Group Guide" for teaching small groups.
- Go to bibledude.net/activistfaith for a list of additional resources and more ways you can get involved.

CHAPTER 3

THE POVERTY EPIDEMIC

WHY WE'RE SICK OF POVERTY (AND WHAT WE'RE DOING TO CHANGE IT)

Dan King

Generous hands are blessed hands because they give bread to the poor.

— Proverbs 22:9 (MSG)

If you see some brother or sister in need and have the means to do something about it but turn a cold shoulder and do nothing, what happens to God's love?

— 1 John 3:17 (MSG)

We're standing in Irene's secondhand clothing shop in the Thika district of Kenya (just outside of Nairobi). The shop itself is approximately a ten-by-ten-foot space that closely resembles the average self-storage unit back home. The walls and ceiling are covered with clothing on hangers in an effort to make it easy for a potential customer to see her entire inventory. She specializes in sweat suits and other workout clothes. But when it comes down to it, she'd sell whatever clothing and accessories she can make a few Kenyan shillings on.

She explains to us how her business works. Every once in a while she takes public transportation into Nairobi to check out incoming shipments of clothing. It mostly comes in from European organizations that take clothing donations from people who are cleaning out their closets.

The clothing comes in bundles, and buyers like her aren't allowed to inspect what's in the bundle; they just buy it and hope for the best. The best she can do is see the general type of clothing from observing the outside of the bundle. But if she gets a bunch of stuff that simply doesn't work for her store, she'll work with other second-hand clothing operators to either sell or swap items, allowing them all to focus on their niches.

Irene is quite proud of her little shop. She works hard to offer quality clothing, run a clean shop, and provide good service to her customers. Her husband works in a local factory but barely makes enough money for their family to survive.

We're all impressed by what Irene is able to do with what she has. You see, Irene is a member of a savings and microcredit group supported by her local church. She worked hard and saved little bits of money the group would pool together and then loan to members who needed it to start or expand a business. She uses the loans she received to help purchase the bundles of clothing that make up her inventory.

After she explains to us how her operation works, we ask her some questions. My biggest question is the same for everyone we meet: "How has the opportunity to run this business with the support of the microloans affected you and your family personally?" She responds simply, "Now I have some extra money to buy things for my kids." She has three children under the age of ten.

This is a response I can really relate to! I have a six-year-old son at home. As his dad, I love having a little extra money from time to time so I can buy something special for him, such as a handheld gaming system. But I don't see many kids around there playing on handheld gaming systems. In most parts of Kenya, handheld gaming system usually means a stick. Some of the more fortunate kids I see get to play with an old, flat soccer ball.

So I ask her, "What kinds of things do you buy for your kids?" She shrugs a little bit and responds, "You know, meat and bread."

For the first time ever in my life, I am utterly speechless. Here I am thinking of all the luxuries I'm going to shower my son with when I return home, and she just told me that all of her hard work provides her the luxury of buying her kids food! This moment has become a defining one in my life and instantly gives my trip to Africa more meaning and purpose than I ever would have expected. What did Irene (and many others like her) do before she had an opportunity like this?

THE EPIDEMIC

Merriam-Webster defines hunger this way:

- A craving or urgent need for food or a specific nutrient
- An uneasy sensation occasioned by the lack of food
- A weakened condition brought about by prolonged lack of food[1]

The Food and Agriculture Organization reports that in 2010, approximately 925 million people lived in a state of hunger.[2] That's nearly three times the population of the United States, which is the third-largest country by population in the world. Can you imagine that?

It's also important to point out that the world has enough resources to feed every person on the planet. This indicates that the principal cause of hunger is poverty. Many people don't have either the quality of land required to produce food or the financial means to purchase it from elsewhere.

What impact does this have on society? The World Health Organization reports that malnutrition poses the single-greatest threat to the world's public health.[3] It drastically increases the risk of infection and infectious disease. Poor nutrition in developing countries has resulted in higher rates of tuberculosis, cardiovascular disease, anemia, and a whole slew of other diseases, not to mention that malnutrition (particularly when it results in iodine deficiency) is a common cause of mental deficiency and other common psychological disorders.

Many of the other problems in the world today have their root in poverty as well. The high number of orphans is largely related to poverty because poverty often leads to uncontrollable disease and higher mortality rates. Many parents of these children simply don't have the means to care and provide for their children. Additionally, most human trafficking and sex slavery victims are from poverty-stricken areas, as individuals are either sold by their own families or tricked while trying to break away from the bondage of poverty.

God's call to us to work in this area is littered throughout the Scriptures. You can start almost anywhere in the Bible and see that God's heart breaks for the poor and that He doesn't want us to cling to "our" resources for ourselves (see Leviticus 19:9-11; Deuteronomy 15:11; Psalm 82:3-4; Matthew 25:37-40).

The kicker is that not only are we called to care for the poor but it's entirely within our ability to fix this. We as the church have the resources to deal with this issue and as a result to help solve many of the other problems we face today. Because it's not a question of quantity of resources, the solution lies more in the distribution of them.

MICROFINANCE: HELPING OR HURTING?

There are lots of organizations out there these days that offer microfinance. It's a pretty simple idea, really, but one that can pack a big punch when it's done right. The simple explanation is that people like Irene can get a small (micro) loan to support small entrepreneurial business development. The result is additional family income that can literally make or break the livelihood of the entire family.

Organizations such as Kiva, ACCION, Grameen, and Five Talents have been working for years to empower people in this way by providing microloans. Often these loans can be for as little as fifty or one hundred dollars. However, microloans can come in many different forms and from different sources, including profit-hungry banks only looking to make a buck and unscrupulous loan sharks who don't care about the loan recipient's success. That's part of the reason microfinance has come under some fire in recent years. However, being critical of microfinance as a poverty alleviation tool is akin to throwing the baby out with the bathwater.

The truth is that there are lots of people out there doing it right. Not everyone is charging unrealistic interest rates; some organizations actually work to help the people succeed in business.

Consider Professor Muhammad Yunus of Bangladesh. He was jointly awarded the Nobel Peace Prize with Grameen Bank in 2006 for their work in fighting poverty. Since then, Bangladesh has seen more than ten million people rise above the $1.25-per-day income poverty threshold, largely due to microfinance.[4]

And you can't write about microfinance without talking about Jacqueline Novogratz, the founder and CEO of Acumen Fund. Novogratz and Acumen Fund impact tens of millions of lives every year by leveraging the entrepreneurial spirit of those in the most poverty-stricken places in the world.

But the fact that there are honest people working hard to implement ethical microfinance programs doesn't by itself mean that it's actually making the difference it's intended to make. Can a loan by itself guarantee a successful lift out of poverty? To answer this question, I think we need to look at the motives of the one doing the lending.

Obviously, the loan sharks and banks that have no interest in seeing people succeed only create situations in which people are set up to fail. Their motivation for profit and control over the borrower results in not only the recipient's financial poverty but also their loss of self-worth and renewed feelings of hopelessness that perpetuate the situation.

The good microfinance organizations do what they can to keep interest rates low. While showing that the organization is less interested in making a quick buck, they also make a loud statement that their focus is on the borrower and not the shareholder.

The great microfinance organizations also do more to help the borrower succeed by implementing educational programs. People are hungry for the training that organizations such as Five Talents offer. I was able to teach basic Christian business principles with Five Talents in Uganda. When profit margins aren't a concern but educational programs and support are, you're probably looking at a microfinance organization that is helping to transform lives and entire communities.

TRANSFORMING LIVES, TRANSFORMING COMMUNITIES

While in Kenya with Five Talents, I had the opportunity to check out the work of the program in place there through a Five Talents partner called Thika Community Development Trust (TCDT). They acted not as a lending institution but rather as a support mechanism for the people running the program themselves.

The way it worked was that a small group of people would come together and save their money. At first it might be ten or twenty people each only bringing in a dollar or two (actually Kenyan shillings). But as the group grew and money was consistently added into the savings pool, loans could start going out.

The group governed itself, electing officers to help oversee activity and manage the group meetings. When someone had saved enough money, they could come to the group and ask for a loan. In order to qualify for a loan, the member would need to have already saved (through the group) at least 50 percent of the value of the loan. So if you wanted a fifty-dollar loan, you must already have at least twenty-five dollars of savings with the group.

Groups like this also keep the interest rates low, usually at 1 or 2 percent just to cover administrative costs associated with keeping the records of activity within the group.

Five Talents never funds the actual group savings, meaning that they do not create a reliance on Western support in order to make the loan programs possible. Instead, they provide administrative support. In addition, teams like ours visit the savings group members to provide training of skills that will help them make the most of their opportunities.

One of my most shocking discoveries about these groups was that more than 99 percent of the repayments were on time. Reportedly, there would occasionally be clients who were a little late on making their payments, but they would eventually be caught up. Effectively, these groups were seeing a 100 percent repayment rate, with more than 99 percent of those payments coming in on time!

It's apparent that the people in groups like this understand the value. Groups have grown steadily, with some of them boasting several hundred members, and provided numerous microloans at any given time.

The self-governance of these successful groups also extends their reach well beyond the microloan business. I remember hearing about one group member leading his group so effectively that he eventually got elected to public government office. Not bad for someone who joined a savings group with a couple of dollars, hoping to someday pull himself out of poverty. Now he's helping push public policy that will continue to help others like him in his community.

A REAL SUCCESS STORY

If you want to really gauge the success of programs like this, I mean *really* gauge their success, it's important to look beyond the direct impact on the clients of these programs. Repayment levels and income statistics are important, but reach is more important. Often the focus of support is too shallow, only targeting the immediate need of an individual. The real success comes when the reach of a program extends well beyond the initial recipient.

While in Kenya, I met a glove maker named Boniface. He started making gloves for a living with the help of a microloan. His specialty was work gloves, especially the kind used in the fields while picking pineapples. Over time, he landed a pretty major contract making gloves for Del Monte, who supplied them to their workers in the pineapple fields. It was an ongoing contract that required regular fulfillment of large quantities of gloves.

The demand got high enough that Boniface had to hire other people to help him make the gloves. Today he employs eight people and has expanded his operation to include two shops in the local market, one where the gloves are made and the other to store them until delivery.

Boniface is very passionate about his employees. He sees what he's doing as an opportunity to not only help others make a little money but also teach them a trade, so he spends time with his employees helping them perfect their craft.

He also encourages them to save a small portion of their money in one of the TCDT savings groups. His dream is that each of his employees would be able to save and eventually get their own loans so that they can start their own glove-making businesses. He says that the market is big enough for many more glove makers, and rather than try to expand much further beyond his means, he'd rather see others learn, grow, and realize the same success he has. The reach of the microloan Boniface received to start his glove-making business has extended well beyond him as the sole beneficiary.

I think some of my favorite success stories are those of the children of microfinance. Before I ever traveled to Africa with Five Talents, I republished some of their stories on my blog. Kelli Ross, the former director of communications for Five Talents, wrote some amazing stories of the kids. One of my favorites is of Fernando in Bolivia:

María, Fernando's mom, started a knitting business in Tarija, Bolivia, with the help of a Five Talents partner, Semillas de Bendición (Seeds of Blessing), in order to provide her four children with nutritious food and clothing. The first loan she received was for $14.

"She had great talent in knitting, but her self-esteem was very low, so we encouraged her to start a business," said Sara and Eva Mamani, Semillas de Bendición program managers. "She was quite fearful, but she decided to take a risk because the poverty in her family was very great. Now, she sells beautiful wool ponchos, and her husband is pleased because their sons are the ones who benefit the most."

Before starting her business, María consistently reminded her sons that she couldn't afford to buy them clothes, school supplies and sometimes even food. Fernando was wearing shoes and a shirt he had outgrown. "My feet were hurting a lot because my shoes were very old, and my shirt for school was very small — it looked like my younger brother's shirt," he said.

Now, María is using her business profits to better provide for her children — one son at a time.

"My mom told me that next time she's not going to buy anything for me since it will be my younger brother's turn," Fernando said. "She will keep working, and she will buy other things for my brothers with what she earns, and they will be happy."

Through her savings group, María has also learned about health and nutrition. "Our mom surprises us with all the yummy things that she cooks; my favorite food is a vegetable cake that she makes," Fernando said.

Now, when 9-year-old Fernando grows up, he wants to be a teacher and a church pastor so that he can help people too.[5]

This is one of my favorite stories for many reasons. We see how one of María's biggest problems was lack of self-esteem, not lack of physical resources. It was such a small loan that made a difference for her as she was encouraged by others to use her talents. But the best part is what's happened in Fernando's life. He doesn't have the same self-esteem problems that his mother struggled with, and because of how his life was influenced at an early age due to his mother's experience, Fernando will extend the impact of that fourteen-dollar loan through generations. The reach of the small financial support spread well beyond the initial recipient.

USING OUR TALENTS

The thing that continues to amaze me about fighting poverty is that it's not as much about money as about talent. We see that in the stories of people like María. However, we also see it in the lives of the activists working in the fight against poverty.

The team I was with in Kenya and Uganda was a Business as Mission team from Five Talents. Through Business as Mission trips, people who have practical business experience (and success) are sent to provide training for loan clients. It's a fantastic model that provides very real and immediate impact. The business skills being taught are extremely foundational, but considering the average level of education in most of these areas, they are right on target.

The model I saw in Kenya showed me that my American money wasn't really needed to provide the loans. That means the best thing I had to offer the people was my (very privileged level of) education and some encouragement.

We taught basic business plan writing, marketing, financial concepts, and goal setting. By American standards, the concepts would have been easy enough for a middle-school kid starting a lemonade stand or lawn-mowing business to comprehend. But I had to remember that many of the participants in our classes had never completed any level of school and the graduation ceremony after our two-day crash course was their first graduation of any kind.

In two days, how much can someone really learn to be successful in business? The financial portion of the training didn't include advanced accounting concepts such as how to put together a strong balance sheet; rather, it instilled such ideas as the importance of keeping personal money and business money separate. The idea is that the average businessperson in the Western world almost inherently has the knowledge to help someone else in a poverty-stricken area exponentially improve his or her skill set and position in life.

In addition to the skills and knowledge transfer, our mere presence encouraged the people more than I ever expected. We were there, in their villages, because we believed in them. We told them that we knew they could do it. You could see the moods of the students change when we shared these affirmations. The fact that they believed in themselves when we were done with our classes was one of the biggest things that made the whole trip worth it for many of us on that team. I learned that breaking the cycle of poverty has less to do with money than it does with breaking the mindsets that keep people locked into it.

BREAKING THE WELFARE-ENTITLEMENT MENTALITY

Too often programs designed to help break the poverty cycle end up hurting because of how they create a reliance on the helper's resources. American churches send teams out on short-term mission trips to deliver goods or provide a service (for example, building something). But when we leave and return home feeling good about how we just helped someone less fortunate, we end up leaving a void that they may not be able to fill on their own. The end result is an entitlement mentality that never really breaks negative cycles.

The problem is that by not providing the right kinds of training and support, we are putting bandages on something that actually requires thoughtful, well-planned surgery. The church needs to learn to become much more strategic in the kind of support it provides.

I've recently witnessed the work of another wonderful

organization, LoveServes International. Currently, LoveServes works on breaking the poverty cycle and welfare-entitlement mentality primarily in the Dominican Republic. They don't try to help by pouring financial and other material resources into the hundreds of indigenous churches they work with; rather, they support local training and mentoring programs designed to teach pastors to go out and transform their own communities.

The church members are taught to look for the needs in their communities and go fill them. Some of the most immediate needs are with helping the elderly and infirm and focusing on poor neighborhood housing conditions. The idea is that when members see a need in their community, they just go out and fill it.

And when the church steps up to meet these needs, many outsiders decide they want to be a part of it. Some of them end up joining the church, while others don't join but continue to help because of the transformation they see happening in their communities. This might be one of the most substantial methods of evangelism I've ever seen. When Christians put the kind of value on other people that Christ puts on each of us, lives are inevitably changed.

One pastor told me that his church members don't wait for outside resources to come in; they just do whatever they can with what they have. This approach certainly limits the extent of what they can do, but they somehow always find enough to take care of the needs in front of them.

Another pastor told me that when they have needs for these community projects, they turn to the kitchens of the people in the church. Church members and other neighbors make baked goods that can be sold in the local markets, and the profits can fund these community transformation projects. Yep, you read that right. The church is engaging in "secular" business activity in order to fund community-development projects.

These pastors are not only seeing their communities transform and their churches grow but are also experiencing a revival in their own walk with Christ. Many are finding new passion and purpose in themselves as they watch God break the bondage of poverty in their communities.

The 750-plus churches LoveServes works with in the Dominican Republic don't rely on U.S. resources. That means there's no welfare mentality. The people learn they can do this with little to no outside help, and they feel even better about that approach in the end.

HOW YOU CAN HELP

It seems the key to fighting poverty is to train, empower, and encourage local ministries and individuals. Getting started in this fight can be overwhelming, but I remember what our Five Talents Business as Mission team leader told us. He talked about how easy it is to get overwhelmed by the enormity of the need. What we need to do (like Nehemiah rebuilding the walls in Jerusalem) is focus on the piece that's right in front of us. If we all cover our part of the wall, together we'll accomplish something great.

On the ActivistFaith.org website, we'll continue to work to provide the kinds of tools and resources that will help you sort through the organizations doing great work in this and many other areas.

For starters though, here is a short list of some of the things you can do with the organizations mentioned in this chapter:

- **Go on a Business as Mission trip.** Education is a big need in underdeveloped countries, and several organizations, such as Five Talents (Five Talents.org), have trips that you can go on to share your business expertise and help budding entrepreneurs launch their small businesses.
- **Support (or host) local job fairs and job skill training programs.** The job skills needed internationally are also needed in our local communities. Google local organizations that hold job fairs and conduct job skills training and find out

where those needs are. Or host a seminar at your church to help people get established in the job market. Not only could you teach technical skills but you could also host résumé-writing and interviewing courses, offering them free to the community.

- **Turn consumerism into an act of charity.** Create a personal giving fund at PureCharity.com and back projects worldwide. Shop through the rewards network to get a percentage back toward your giving fund. Share projects with your friends and earn more when they sign up.
- **Host a 30-hour famine.** Churches, and especially students, may be drawn to this event that raises awareness of world hunger and helps participants contribute to a solution as they experience hunger themselves.
- **Fund a microloan.** Kiva (Kiva.org) has a great setup that allows you to choose a borrower, make a loan, get repaid, and repeat!

This is by no means a complete list, but it shows the variety of ways you can have an impact. The good news is there's a great deal that can be done to break the poverty cycle, and it's a battle that can be won by focusing on the right things.

THINK IT THROUGH

Take a few minutes to digest what you've learned and answer the following questions. If you're reading this as a group, talk through your thoughts together.

1. Take an inventory of the skills and resources you (individually or as a group) have that could be used for supporting others who need job skill training and development. What talents do you have that can be useful to

others?

2. Talk with your church's missions or outreach person/team about where there may be opportunities to offer the kind of training that you feel prepared to conduct. Where are the needs that are already connected to your church?
3. If there are no easy connections already within your church, what are the local (or international) organizations that could use your help?
4. How can you rally others to support a microenterprise solution? Consider all the tools at your disposal, such as social media and church groups and activities.

HELPFUL TOOLS AND RESOURCES

For Research

- *The Unlikely Missionary: From Pew-Warmer to Poverty-Fighter*, by Dan King (BibleDude Press, 2011)
- *When Helping Hurts: How to Alleviate Poverty Without Hurting the Poor . . . and Yourself*, by Brian Fikkert and Steve Corbett (Moody, 2009)
- *Following Jesus Through the Eye of the Needle: Living Fully, Loving Dangerously*, by Kent Annan (InterVarsity, 2009)

For Action

- Visit LoveServes International (LoveServes.org), AccionUSA .org, and GrameenFoundation.org for more opportunities to serve.
- Go to bibledude.net/activistfaith to join others in the fight against poverty.

CHAPTER 4

CREATED TO CARE

A BALANCED APPROACH TO ENVIRONMENTALISM

Dillon Burroughs

God saw everything that He had made, and indeed it was very good.

— Genesis 1:31 (NKJV)

Humanity began with life in a garden. Adam and Eve existed in a land of trees, plants, and wildlife untouched by modern development. It was there they experienced a deep relationship with God, one another, and the world around them.

In fact, God called His creation "good" on multiple occasions in Genesis 1. From the seas to plant life to animal life and even human life, each facet was blessed with the touch of the Creator's handiwork, displaying beauty, creativity, and diversity.

Human sin led to life outside of Eden, but it did not end God's care for creation.

Today we face the growing dilemma of a world whose God-given beauty meets the contamination of human exploitation. Rain forests disappear to meet consumer demands. Animal habitats face endangerment or extinction due to the extraction of energy resources. Modern landfills and waste contaminate water supplies and soil, leaving devastating consequences on all forms of life: plant, animal, and human.

Alexei Laushkin wrote,

> Climate change won't go away, it's a pressing need. If people don't have access to clean air, clean water, and a stable food supply they aren't able to build free prosperous societies. It just won't happen. Climate change impacts the ability for the least of these to have access to food and water. The type of energy we use matters; it matters to those who have to live with the consequences of pollution.[1]

As we consider the great social issues of our time, we would be unwise to overlook the tremendous need to address our changing environment. We can debate global warming, but our duty to care for God's creation is clear.

Our duty? How can I be sure? I recently read an article that asked if Christians can be environmentalists. Blow by blow, each side produced its reasons for and against this question as if the issue were up for debate. But here is what is really at stake:

1. Christians believe that God created the earth.
2. Genesis says God called it good.

For those of us who call ourselves Christians, how are we to treat things God calls good? The simple answer is that we better care a lot about what God calls good. God called people "good," animals "good," and a whole list of virtues, the church, and especially His Son Jesus "good." We are called to treat these areas of life with the utmost respect. Why would we treat the environment any differently?

As a kid, I cared about what my dad cared about, whether it was his favorite baseball team (the Yankees) or his favorite food (popcorn). When our heavenly Father calls something good, the idea is that His kids will treat it with respect, caring about it like He does.

Some have found the idea of caring for the environment as

somehow condoning nature worship or even idolatry. But this is simply untrue. As the Evangelical Environmental Network noted,

> At the same time that we condemn nature worship, we must not let our zeal to avoid idolatry prevent us from our biblical call to care for all of creation. Indeed, one cannot fully worship the Creator and at the same time destroy His creation, which was brought into being to glorify him. Worshiping the Creator and caring for creation is all part of loving God. They are mutually reinforcing activities. It is actually unbiblical to set one against the other.[2]

So should Christians care about the environment? Yes! Let's begin by taking a quick look at five principles Scripture teaches about God's creation:

1. **Both animal life and human life reflect God's creative power:**

> Ask the animals, and they will teach you,
> or the birds of the air, and they will tell you;
> or speak to the earth, and it will teach you,
> or let the fish of the sea inform you.
> Which of all these does not know
> that the hand of the LORD has done this?
> In his hand is the life of every creature
> and the breath of all mankind. (Job 12:7-10, NIV)

2. **The sky points to God's glory:**

> The heavens declare the glory of God;
> the skies proclaim the work of his hands.
> Day after day they pour forth speech;
> night after night they display knowledge.

There is no speech or language
where their voice is not heard.
Their voice goes out into all the earth,
their words to the ends of the world. (Psalm 19:1-4, NIV)

3. Creation was God's first missionary:

Ever since the creation of the world his eternal power and divine nature, invisible though they are, have been understood and seen through the things he has made. So they are without excuse. (Romans 1:20)

4. Nature brings praise to God:

Praise the LORD from the heavens,
praise him in the heights above.
Praise him, all his angels,
praise him, all his heavenly hosts.
Praise him, sun and moon,
praise him, all you shining stars.
Praise him, you highest heavens
and you waters above the skies.
Let them praise the name of the LORD,
for he commanded and they were created.
He set them in place for ever and ever;
he gave a decree that will never pass away. (Psalm 148:1-6, NIV)

5. Nature is both created and controlled by God:

Praise the LORD from the earth,
you great sea creatures and all ocean depths,
lightning and hail, snow and clouds,
stormy winds that do his bidding,

> you mountains and all hills,
> fruit trees and all cedars,
> wild animals and all cattle,
> small creatures and flying birds. (Psalm 148:7-10, NIV)

As Christian environmental activist Ben Lowe said,

> The thinking that "the earth is ours and revolves around us" must shift to an authentic appreciation that "the earth is God's and revolves around Him." Lifestyles, which are insulated from the natural consequences that they have on creation and our neighbors, must be transformed in order to live more compassionately toward all that God has made. Cultures which value being over-busy and over-productive must learn to make room for community and Sabbath rest. A mistrust of science, based on a belief that it's a secular discipline that tries to disprove God, must be relinquished. Rather, science must be viewed as a spiritual discipline that helps us uncover more about how God created and sustains life to flourish and bring Him glory. Finally, we must let go of the false dichotomy that caring for the environment comes at the expense of caring for people. Christians are meant to embrace a much more holistic paradigm, specifically that caring for people and the planet are integrally connected.[3]

HOW THE ENVIRONMENT AFFECTS US ALL

As I researched material for this chapter, I discovered one serious way in which issues of the environment affect us: the mercury poisoning of the unborn. According to the Evangelical Environmental Network, one in six babies—more than 700,000 each year—are born with harmful levels of mercury in their blood, and coal-burning power plants are the largest source of domestic mercury pollution.[4] This is an urgent and escalating moral crisis that calls for immediate action!

But what can we do? We can start by going to the Evangelical Environmental Network's website (CreationCare.org) and signing up for their ongoing updates. I did and encourage you to as well. This is a great first step as a public commitment to doing your part to care for God's created world. Second, you can use the resources on the site to find contact information to e-mail, write, or call your local representatives and senators as well as the Environmental Protection Agency to ask them to speak out on the topic. For those with concerns about mercury in their food, the website also offers a "Mercury Free Shopping Guide" to consider (available for free at http://creationcare.org/media.php?what=21).

HOW YOU CAN HELP

You want to help lessen your negative impact on the environment but don't know how? What follows are some ideas for your personal benefit as well as ones you may find useful for your church community or workplace. What you'll discover is that many believers are leading the way in improving the environmental situation, something you can join starting today.

- **Look at what you throw away (REDUCE).** According to the Environmental Protection Agency, the average American produces about 4.4 pounds of garbage a day, or a total of 29 pounds per week and 1,600 pounds a year. The garbage produced in America could form a line of garbage trucks that reaches the moon![5] If we want to create environmental change, the place to start is with what we waste.

  Last year I attempted a personal experiment I called "The Zero Trash Week." For one week, I made it my goal to create zero trash in my office. Instead, I would purchase only products that could be recycled, including food, drinks, and office supplies. Believe it or not, it was possible to make it five working days without a single scrap of trash! Since then, I still throw away items when needed, but I estimate that I now produce at least 60 percent less office waste.

Another great way to reduce is to cut back on unnecessary uses of electricity. From leaving off the lights to unplugging unused electronics, such actions greatly help in reducing how much energy is consumed. For example, that cell phone charger you left plugged in at home still uses power even when not connected to your phone. One charger times the number of cell phone chargers in use in our world right now could likely run your city's power needs for the day (or maybe a week).

One big change we made at our house several years ago was to buy paper towels that separate in smaller sections. We have not converted to all cloth hand towels, but we are reducing our impact. How? A decrease in U.S. household consumption of just three rolls of paper towels per year would save 120,000 tons of waste and $4.1 million in landfill dumping fees.[6] That's a lot of trash!

Here's one not everyone likes but that really does work: Flush one less time per day (not recommended for the office!). If every American flushed just one less time per day, we could save up to 219 trillion gallons of water per year! That's a small change to make, considering the nearly one billion people on earth who completely lack access to clean water.[7]

Finally, consider your driving habits. According to the committee Environment@rtp, if the average commuter carpooled every day, he or she would save five hundred gallons of gasoline and 550 pounds of poisonous exhaust emissions every year.[8] I know some families that have five people who drive five different vehicles to church on Sunday.

What message does this send about our concern for the environment? And whenever possible, get some exercise when you travel. Biking or walking to a destination is better for your health and doesn't pollute the air we all breathe.

- **Look at what you can use again (REUSE).** Americans love the latest and greatest gadgets. Women obsess over new shoes and purses. Guys prefer the latest big screen or mobile phone. But simply reusing what we have or buying secondhand items helps lessen the impact we have in producing unnecessary waste.

  For example, consider our nation's use of food leftovers. It has been said by some experts that America throws away enough food to feed every starving person in the world. I don't know if this is true, but many of us leave behind a pile of food for disposal every time we eat at a restaurant. The same is often similar with our meals at home. With a little effort, we can reduce our food waste by 15 to 20 percent just by better use of the food we already have. *Time* writer Brad Tuttle explained, "The suggested acronym is MSR, as in Make more than you need, Save the extras, and Repurpose those extras later."[9] I know this one from experience. We've been practicing it at home ever since having kids. Another benefit: It saves money on groceries.

  Clothing is another great example. If every American donated one clothing item per person to those in need, it would increase available clothing for 300 *million* people without a single new piece of clothing produced.

  Bottled drinks are another big underutilized area. The booming bottled water and plastic bottled drink markets have literally produced billions of empty bottles. Though these can be recycled, many can be avoided altogether. Using reusable water bottles is one of the top ways to reduce the use of plastic.

  Plastic bags are another area applicable to nearly every

family. Many experts complain that the bags we use from the local grocery or department store cannot be recycled and damage the environment. However, it helps greatly to simply reuse the same bags more than once. After shopping, my family uses the bags for our smaller trash cans around the house, giving each bag a second life. If it's going in the trash, I want to use it at least one more time to reduce the amount of other plastic bags used. This single practice can also reduce the need to buy additional trash bags for home or office use. One of my favorite stores, a secondhand bookstore called McKay's, uses recycled plastic bags in its business. It's a great fit for a place that already sells used items, and it saves them the additional cost of buying their own bags.

One further step in this area many now take is the use of reusable cloth bags when shopping. This helpful step can cut off many plastic bags before they are even used. Further, many grocers also offer paper bags. Use these whenever possible rather than plastic and then recycle the bags. Yes, trees are used in making paper bags, but this paper is recycled paper that has already been used at least once.

- **Look at what you can recycle (RECYCLE).** As a family, we began recycling a few years ago when we became convicted about the amount of trash we produced. We use Allied Waste's recycling service, which picks up unsorted recycling every other week at our curb in a large green container. Our family has cut the amount of trash we produce by more than 40 percent. That may not sound like much, but if every home in America practiced this, we would likely no longer be the world's top garbage-producing nation.

  Aluminum cans are one of the easiest ways we can all recycle. In many states, these can still earn some money at recycling centers. The important thing is not to throw that can in your hand into the trash. Why not? The aluminum can you throw away today will still be a can one hundred years from now.

Did you know that phone books make up nearly 10 percent of the waste found in landfill sites? Recycle yours or, better yet, call to request that future delivery of phone books to your home be stopped. You can use online computer or mobile phone searches instead, and you'll help save some trees and trash in the process.

Paper is possibly our biggest untapped resource for recycling. Did you realize that to produce each week's Sunday newspapers in America, 500,000 trees must be cut down? If all our newspapers were recycled, we could save about *250 million trees each year*. The average household throws away 13,000 separate pieces of paper each year. Most is packaging and junk mail.[10]

Another good idea for the office, both at home and at work, is to photocopy and print double-sided whenever possible. Did you realize that if even one in four pages we copied or printed each day were double-sided, we would save 130 billion sheets of paper per year? That's a stack thicker than the diameter of the earth![11]

- **Look at how you can live differently (RETHINK).** We've talked about specific actions we can take to improve our impact upon "God's green earth," but what about ways we can live and be different in relation to creation care? This means doing what we can to help personally *and* getting others involved. There are basically two areas you can concentrate on beyond your own home: your church and your place of employment.

    - *At church.* Become part of establishing better policies for recycling and better environmental impact. Volunteer to help start a recycling ministry if necessary. Recycle every aluminum can, scrap of paper, and pizza box your youth group tosses and keep track of how much you recycle. In six months, you'll have a report that shocks your church's members. Plus, you may be able to sell the aluminum cans to generate additional income for service projects or a mission trip.

Second, encourage green policies at your church. Beyond recycling, the number one thing you could target would be the use of Styrofoam for church functions. Replace Styrofoam cups and plates with paper made from post-consumer materials. Replace napkins in your church kitchen with ones made from recycled materials. Work to reduce unnecessary use of heat and air conditioning during unused hours in your building and address lights left on after office hours. Not only will these changes improve environmental impact but you'll likely notice a lower dollar amount on your church's utility bills.

Third, consider the possibility of a community garden on your church's property (or the property of a church member with appropriate land). My own church launched a community garden two years ago. The result? There is now a waiting list for farming plots! Each person or family has a designated section to grow vegetables of their choice. At the beginning of the season, there is a planting day, in which everyone breaks ground and begins. Members talk throughout the summer about their garden and are responsible for watering and weeding, often sharing turns with other members. Friendships blossom as well as plants, all while offering teachable moments to discuss our intimate connection with God's creation.

Fourth, take time to teach about the importance of climate care. This could be done through a brochure or a teaching series or Bible study on the topic. Even using this chapter in your class or group could be a great starting point.

- *At the office.* Because every person's office or workplace is different, all I can recommend here are ideas that might work for your situation. Be creative and you'll find more than what is mentioned here. These are just to get you started.

  As in the church ideas I mentioned, basic recycling is the place to start. One guy named Ben at my office started recycling where I work. That was two years ago. The other day, we had an entire pickup truck of cardboard taken to recycling. Do you think his actions are helping us improve our impact on the environment? Ben is my office recycling hero! Our office is a different place because he took some time to set out different containers for plastic, paper, aluminum cans, and cardboard. It all started with one person who believed that our love for God should extend to how we use our God-given resources.

  Also, kitchen products are easy targets for change. Requesting recycled or post-consumer products at the office can greatly reduce waste. An easy way to start is to donate some appropriate paper items of your own to show how simple the difference can be.

  Office Supply Services' "Green Office Project" offers these guidelines for greener office purchases. First, ask three questions when considering an office purchase: Where does it come from, how is it used, and where will it end up? Some ways to vote with your dollar for positive change are to buy products that are made with post-consumer recycled material, that are biodegradable or compostable, and that reduce chemical content. You might consider purchasing renewable energy (wind- or solar-powered items).[12]

  Look into having your company allow employees to

put a certain number of volunteer hours toward their working hours. If so, a community service project focused on environmental issues could be a good choice. Finally, if your employer allows matching funds to community organizations, consider a place that assists in improving the environment in your community.

- **Be all in.** Some of you reading this might be quite serious about partnering with an organization that serves on the cutting edge of the Christian environmental and climate change movement. If so, there are two places I encourage you to consider.

  First, take a moment to browse the work of Plant with Purpose at PlantwithPurpose.org. Their goal is to address the connection between poverty and the environment. Many people think of poverty and the environment as separate issues, but they are connected. Most of the world's poor are rural poor, depending on farming for their food. Widespread environmental damage means that land does not produce the crops it once did. Plant with Purpose helps the poor restore productivity to their land to create economic opportunity out of environmental restoration.

  In simple terms, Plant with Purpose combines discipleship and environmental efforts into a single ministry. You can purchase trees to reforest a nation and even take a trip to do it yourself. (Plant with Purpose currently operates in more than 250 villages in Haiti, Mexico, Thailand, Burundi, Tanzania, and the Dominican Republic.) Imagine planting trees and working in churches to provide evangelistic events and discipleship. In many developing nations, this holistic approach is key to showing care for their land while also serving spiritual needs.

  A second way to go all in on the environmental issue is through the Young Evangelicals for Climate Action movement, which is part of the larger Evangelical Environmental Network (CreationCare.org). Their stated mission is to be "young evangelicals in the United States who are coming together and taking action to overcome the climate crisis as part of our Christian discipleship and witness." On their website, you can sign their "Call to Action," become a member, and participate in the movement to mobilize young evangelicals toward greater environmental action. In their words,

> In seeking to live as Christ's disciples, we have come to see the climate crisis as a profound threat to "the least of these" (Mt. 25). Therefore, we find it imperative to speak out on behalf of those communities that are marginalized and disempowered, as well as the entire created order that is groaning for its redemption (Rom. 8:23). For us, this is an act of worship and service to our Creator.[13]

Neither of these organizations is a substitute for efforts within a local church, yet they exist as opportunities for those who feel led to greater action and involvement regarding what God is doing among this generation of believers in the area of climate care.

Author Ed Begley Jr. said that when it comes to going green, we should pick the low-hanging fruit first.[14] In other words, each of us can help save the earth by making small, simple changes to our habits and lifestyles. We don't have to sell our homes, donate all our belongings to Goodwill, and move to a hut in the Amazon rain forest. We can have a positive effect on the environment wherever we live, whoever we are, and no matter what we do for a living.

The key is to start small and start now. If you do something and I do something and everyone who reads these words does something to improve our environment, Christians will be known as people who care for God's creation and those who live in it.

THINK IT THROUGH

Take a few minutes to digest what you've learned and answer the following questions. If you're reading this as a group, talk through your thoughts together.

1. Why do you think it's important for Christians to be seen as people who care about the created world? How is creation care an important part of Christian faith?
2. What is a way you can personally begin to take steps to better care for God's creation?
3. How could you involve your family, school, church, or workplace in creation care activities? How could a recycling ministry work in your congregation?

HELPFUL TOOLS AND RESOURCES

For Research

- *Serve God, Save the Planet*, by J. Matthew Sleeth (Zondervan, 2007)
- *The Green Book*, by Elizabeth Rogers and Thomas M. Kostigen (Three Rivers Press, 2007)
- *Living Green*, by Greg Horn (Freedom Press, 2006)

For Action

- Go to bibledude.net/activistfaith to join with others in environmental activism.

CHAPTER 5

EMERGENCY RESPONSE

TAKING THE "DISASTER" OUT OF DISASTER RELIEF

Dan King

Each of us as human beings has a responsibility to reach out to help our brothers and sisters affected by disasters. One day it may be us or our loved ones needing someone to reach out and help.

—Michael W. Hawkins, American Red Cross

Unless someone like you cares a whole awful lot, nothing is going to get better. It's not.

—Dr. Seuss

It started with the simple act of giving things away. As I recall, there's even some free rat bait and cheetah-print nightgowns in the roots of this story. And as word got out that they were the church that gave things away, Healing Place Church in Baton Rouge, Louisiana, found itself in the middle of an unexpected ministry—well, unexpected in the sense that I don't believe anyone would (or could) have planned for it to all go down this way.

When word got out that they were the church that gives stuff away, donations of items to give away started rolling in from area businesses. Then just as quickly as the goods came in, the church turned around and started sharing them with people in the community.

When a church starts operating like this, it doesn't take long to put the correct systems in place to manage these initiatives. And once that is done, relationships with the community and area businesses quickly develop too. The goal for Healing Place Church was always to express the love of Jesus in a practical way in the community, and the strategy was working.

Then on September 11, 2001, terrorism struck New York City and Washington, D.C. With thousands dead or missing and exponentially more in shock over the tragedy, the church knew it was time to demonstrate the love of Jesus once again. They knew they had to respond—and respond quickly. Within forty-eight hours of the attacks, they had two of their pastors at Ground Zero to find out from the firemen what the needs were. With a phone call back to the church, the community immediately began loading semitrailers with the requested supplies.

Through this experience, Healing Place Church learned a lot about expecting the unexpected and being prepared for anything. You never know when crisis will strike, and having the systems in place to respond quickly has become a cornerstone for how the church operates. And it's a good thing, because just a few years after their 9/11 response efforts, they were hit a little closer to home.

On August 29, 2005, the levees in New Orleans broke under the pressure of Hurricane Katrina. The storm put 80 percent of New Orleans under as much as fifteen feet of water. Healing Place Church's pastor, Dino Rizzo, recalled the full story of the church's reaction to the crisis in his book *Servolution*. In it, he stated, "Nothing could have prepared us for the awful images flooding the airwaves, but there was one thing we *were* prepared to do: respond."[1]

Rizzo talked about how moved he was to see the ways his church partnered with several of the local churches to provide shelter for people and minister to the physical, emotional, and spiritual needs of the victims of the crisis.

THE CHURCH AS A CRISIS CENTER

"Prayer changes things." That's what Romanita Hairston, vice president of World Vision's U.S. Programs, says about responding to disasters. When disaster strikes, World Vision is quick to get on location to help provide essential supplies during the initial recovery phase. World Vision is very focused on partnering primarily with local churches as they assess and establish long-term recovery efforts. Why churches? Because it's the church that people look to when they need healing and hope after suffering from a traumatic experience. And when many people begin the recovery process after a disaster, they often look to God for strength.

When I spoke to Romanita in the aftermath of the 2011 Super Outbreak of tornadoes that hit Joplin, Missouri, and parts of Alabama, she talked about the role of the church in recovery efforts:

> The grace of God is that He shows up in the midst of it. He shows up during it, and He's there afterwards. And really what the faith community is doing in Joplin is showing up as God's hands and feet to demonstrate His love, and to help raise that voice that God was there when it happened. He was sparing lives and saving people, and the Spirit of the Lord was intervening. And that's going to continue as Joplin moves forward.[2]

The church has always been a center of community, and there's good reason for that. When crisis strikes in people's lives, it's often the church that brings the healing that's needed. The organization of the church becomes a great vehicle for distribution of goods and other basic needs, but it's the deeper aspects that make people show up. They come because they often struggle to make sense of the crisis event. This means that the church is uniquely positioned to have the greatest impact with all types of needs in the wake of disaster.

SPIRITUALITY AND OVERCOMING DISASTER

When I think about major disasters such as the 2004 Indian Ocean earthquake and tsunami or the 2010 Haiti earthquake, it's easy to see the impact of major losses. Images of people walking around dazed and confused, wondering where their lost loved ones might be, filled media channels and social media sites. The damage of these disasters wasn't merely the loss of something physical like a car or even a house; many in these situations experienced loss in magnitudes that most of us can never imagine.

One study published in 2004 in the *Oxford Journals* had this to say about disasters and their victims:

> Disasters are mass traumatic events that involve multiple persons and are frequently accompanied by loss of property and economic hardship on a large scale. As such, there may be a wide range of people who may be considered "victims" of a disaster, including those who nearly escape death, those who are injured, family members of the deceased, and those who witness a catastrophic event.[3]

The study continued by pointing out that victims of these disasters are at high risk of suffering post-traumatic stress disorder (PTSD):

> Studies conducted in the aftermath of disasters during the past 40 years have shown that there is a substantial burden of PTSD among persons who experience a disaster.[4]

I'll talk more about PTSD in another chapter, but these deep levels of brokenness can require deep healing. Often people who suffer from PTSD struggle to make sense of the traumatic events they've just experienced. When this happens, people with a strong faith system typically find it easier to cope with the events and find peace with losses they experienced.

One great example of this is the story of the church in the Petionville tent city that formed after the 2010 earthquake. One of the big celebrity advocates who responded was actor Sean Penn. Almost immediately after the earthquake, Penn packed his bags and headed for Haiti. The amazing thing about this is that although he could have stayed in some of the more comfortable lodging places, he chose to move into a tent in Haiti's largest tent city.

Even Penn, who is not a Christ follower, recognized the strong spiritual nature of the Haitian people. He knew that one of the best things that could be done would be to find a spiritual leader for the community of now-homeless earthquake survivors. Enter Pastor Jean St. Cyr, a Haitian pastor who, despite having the means to leave, made the difficult decision to stay in Haiti and minister to his people. Penn and St. Cyr worked together to establish a tent church in the middle of the tent city. And ever since, the church has become a place of healing and restoration for many who still live in the tents, years after the earthquake.

IT'S NOT JUST FOR NATURAL DISASTERS

In the Healing Place Church story, we see that disaster relief isn't exclusive to just natural disasters. Man-made disasters, such as the 9/11 attacks, create the same sense of loss that natural disasters cause. The questions regarding why can differ a little, but the shock value and impact can be very much the same. Some estimates indicate that the number of PTSD cases in New York City after the attacks were over four hundred thousand.[5] Incidentally, alcohol, cigarette, and marijuana use were all up significantly, as were sales in sex stores as people searched for ways to cope with the stress and trauma. Church and synagogue attendance was up significantly but not as much as alcohol and sex store sales.

The bottom line is that no matter the cause of the disaster, people are searching for ways to cope with the impact and meaning of the event. With man-made disasters, there is the additional element of knowing who caused the event, so not only do survivors struggle with the loss of loved ones but they must also process the anger being directed at those who caused the tragedy.

WHAT IT MEANS TO CARE FOR OUR NEIGHBORS

It would be great if one of the Ten Commandments clearly stated something along the lines of "Thou shalt provide emergency relief for victims of disasters." But as you know, the Bible isn't always that direct on certain issues. However, it's not a stretch to see a theme as it relates to caring for our brothers, especially when there's some kind of need.

This is actually one of my favorite marks of the early church. They had a strong desire to go and help people in need, even at risk to themselves. I've heard that during times of plague, many people typically fled to avoid the sickness, and often it was the Christians who would stay and provide basic care to help people recover. It's been said that this kind of selflessness is one of the big reasons for the large number of converts in the first few centuries of Christianity. This kind of love resonates deeply with survivors today as well and becomes an effective evangelism tool.

There's a great deal of biblical support for this idea of loving your neighbors and caring for their needs. Of all the passages I could talk about here, I want to focus on four that represent key ideas to guide us in our efforts.

Anticipation and Outflow in the Early Church

Pay attention to Paul's words here:

> Some prophets came down from Jerusalem to Antioch. One of them, named Agabus, stood up and through the Spirit predicted

> that a severe famine would spread over the entire Roman world. (This happened during the reign of Claudius.) The disciples, each according to his ability, decided to provide help for the brothers living in Judea. This they did, sending their gift to the elders by Barnabas and Saul. (Acts 11:27-30, NIV)

There are three important concepts covered in this passage. Each of these elements is crucial when it comes to building a disaster relief plan. First, the church was guided by the Word of the Lord. The foundation of every good disaster relief plan is that it's founded in prayer. Every church is uniquely equipped to provide different types of resources. It's important to use the strengths God has blessed your church with. The church in Antioch had prophets who predicted the coming disaster, and therefore the church was able to prepare ahead of time in order to minimize the impact. We might not know when or where something like an earthquake or hurricane is going to hit, but we can know ahead of time how we can respond and support those most affected. So pray and ask God to show you how you can help others and how you can be ready.

Second, when the church was made aware of the impending disaster, their response was to help in whatever way they could. It's not something God told them they had to do; rather, it was something they decided to do, knowing that their brothers and sisters in Christ were going to be suffering. It was the natural reaction of these disciples, and it should be the natural reaction of disciples today.

Lastly, it's also worth noting where the help being offered was sent. It's the same structure we see modeled today by organizations like World Vision. The support was provided to the local churches in the affected areas. It wasn't sent to other groups or organizations, and they didn't go establish their own presence in the community. Instead, they operated behind the scenes and worked through and strengthened the local church leadership so that the local (indigenous) church could be the source of relief for its own community.

Remembering to Serve Fellow Believers

> While we have opportunity, let us do good to all people, and especially to those who are of the household of the faith. (Galatians 6:10, NASB)

This is a tricky one. Often people look at this verse and think that Christians should help only Christians or at least put most of their effort into helping all Christians. But there are two parts to this statement. First, it is stated that we are to "do good to *all* people," and then it's stated that we should pay particular attention to those in "the household of the faith."

Let's start with talking about "the household of the faith" with this one. Jesus did teach us that it would be by our love for each other that the world would know us. Our care for other Christians should be at a level that turns heads and makes people recognize there's something different about us. It's not the kind of love that kindhearted outsiders would give to an important cause; rather, this is a heavenly love that heals and restores in ways nothing else can. So, yes, in our response to needs that arise, the church should definitely care for its own with a level of excellence the rest of the world rarely sees otherwise.

However, the Christian church was never intended to be an exclusive club. Jesus rebuked the church leaders of His day for this kind of thing (see Matthew 15:22-28; Luke 11:42-43). Everyone is welcome, and our disaster relief efforts should reflect that. "So then, while we have opportunity," we can pour out Christ's love on damaged and hurting communities, bringing healing and restoration even to nonbelievers. This kind of response from the church can be a great evangelistic tool, resulting in many coming to know the Lord because of the unwarranted, unconditional love we've given them—the same kind of love that saved many of us from utter destruction.

The God of All Comfort

Where is God in the midst of our suffering?

> All praise to the God and Father of our Master, Jesus the Messiah! Father of all mercy! God of all healing counsel! He comes alongside us when we go through hard times, and before you know it, he brings us alongside someone else who is going through hard times so that we can be there for that person just as God was there for us. We have plenty of hard times that come from following the Messiah, but no more so than the good times of his healing comfort—we get a full measure of that, too. (2 Corinthians 1:3-4, MSG)

This is a beautiful thing! As Christians, we have been given a life and a hope that others don't have. We've been healed from the inside and have overcome the worst the world has to offer. And for that very reason, we praise! God has blessed us mightily, and our natural response to that blessing is our worship. But the best part is that He allows us to experience that redemptive work in other ways; besides merely receiving it, we can also be vessels of delivering it!

That's what makes this whole thing so amazing. We get to experience a little taste of what God experiences with us. He makes us a part of His redemptive work, and we are able to be part of the healing for others going through difficult times. This honor is something Christians get to experience, and it can be quite rewarding. When we pour out love on hurting communities, we inevitably find ourselves closer to the heartbeat of the God we serve.

Letting Your Light Shine

> Let your light shine before men in such a way that they may see your good works, and glorify your Father who is in heaven. (Matthew 5:16, NASB)

In a world where almost everyone focuses on his or her own needs, we bring glory to God by being a light. Our selfless, humble service to others gives credibility to the gospel we preach; it allows others to see a practical demonstration of the love of God. And when our actions direct attention away from ourselves and bring recognition to Him, we end up practicing evangelism at a level that our words can never reach.

OVERCOMING ABUSE OF THE SYSTEM

When disaster first strikes, there's usually a flood of financial support to help the victims. Organizations are finding much easier ways to provide potential donors a way to give, such as through websites and text messaging. And they've made it both easy and affordable to donate. By simplifying the donation process (as in the case of text-message donations), organizations can leverage the support of large masses of people donating as little as five dollars rather than waiting for large donations few can afford.

Often these campaigns result in literally millions of dollars rolling in within days or even hours of a disaster. At times, organizations can become overwhelmed when the money comes in faster than they can use it. However, a good organization will eventually distribute all the money to the right places.

If you're concerned about choosing a legitimate organization with honest business practices, take a close look at its transparency and track record. There are several organizations in which fraud isn't a question because a great deal of emphasis is placed on providing clear, accurate information to donors and the public regarding the use of funds.

HOW TO RESPOND WHEN DISASTER STRIKES

When responding to disaster, it's always good to have a plan. Post-disaster activity can be hectic enough without scrambling to figure things out as you go, not to mention that disaster recovery isn't an overnight project. Whatever you do, it will take planning, commitment, and wisdom. Here are some steps that will help guide you in developing a disaster recovery plan.

Good emergency response begins before the emergency.

Even before disaster strikes, you should take inventory of *everything.* At any given time, you should know what physical resources you have: food, building supplies, medical supplies. What about financial resources? Do you have an emergency relief fund that could be tapped to help out when it's not practical to send other physical resources?

You should also take inventory of people's talents and skills. What skills do you or others in your church have that could be used in an emergency situation? For example, you might make a list of people who are doctors, nurses, lawyers, pastors, and counselors and those with great organizational skills, to name only a few.

What would it take to move the appropriate resources when disaster strikes? Make sure the resources you have are ready to move when needed. This will allow you to respond the right way at the right time.

Give the help that's needed, not what makes you feel good about yourself.

I had the privilege of visiting a rice-farming community in Haiti approximately two years after the earthquake. Even though the village is well outside the damage area of the disaster, the impact is still being felt as ripples of relief efforts make their way into the country. But the damage there isn't physical; it's economic.

When the earthquake happened, relief efforts by organizations from around the world stepped into high gear. Recognizing the need to get people much-needed food, many aid organizations began shipping rice into Port-au-Prince. The overabundance of foreign rice meant that the local Haitian rice wasn't needed. The sudden decrease in demand for rice from these Haitian rice-farming communities has left many families without the income needed to support themselves.

The moral here is that we need to be very careful and wise about the support we give. Well-meaning organizations never intended to devastate the local economies. And just as organizations need to think through the impacts of the support they bring to emergency response situations, even individuals need to understand the needs of the local communities they're trying to help. In some cases, physical labor is the greatest need. Other times, it may simply be financial support so that those affected can buy the local resources they need.

What disaster victims don't need is the help that *we* think they need. Wise disaster relief planning means that we're not giving whatever makes us feel as though we've contributed; rather, we're investigating and finding a way to supply what helps the victims and their communities the most.

Leverage those who are already equipped to respond.

Depending on the scale of the disaster, there may already be people in place ready to respond. In smaller-scale situations, it will be the first responders—police, firefighters, paramedics, and hospital staff—who take the brunt of the work when something bad happens. Opening the conversation and developing relationships with these people and organizations in your area does two things. First, it gives you a connection to finding out what the greatest needs are at any given time. Second, it lets the first responders know who you are and what you can do when they need some sort of support. Keep in mind that your community involvement before disaster strikes strengthens your credibility as a resource when the need arises.

This method of preparation isn't limited to local resources. Organizations like World Vision and the Red Cross are regularly active in emergency situations, and you and your church can become strong partners for these kinds of organizations, helping them provide the best response they can offer.

The bottom line here is that we shouldn't need to reinvent the wheel when it comes to responding to disaster. There are people and organizations already in place who are on the front lines of disaster relief, and often the greatest thing we can do is be a support for whatever they need.

If you have local connections, work through them to meet needs and support local leadership.

When the emergency isn't in your area, it's important to make sure you're working through local contacts and leadership. If your church has denominational ties, find the local denominational church in that area and offer your help through their leadership team. If your church doesn't have those kinds of connections, try to find another like-minded church to partner with or check with other parachurch organizations that you partner with to find out if they're already working in the affected region.

The goal of a good disaster relief plan isn't to show your presence there but rather to strengthen the efforts of local leadership. Think about what it would be like if a storm passed through and devastated your community. How would you feel if some other church without ties to your community set up camp at the vacant lot just down the road from your church and offered help to the people in your community? Wouldn't you rather they partnered with your church and helped support your efforts in your own community?

If there's one thing Jesus has taught me, it's that it's not my goal to make myself famous. My goal is always to make someone else famous–namely, Him—and that requires a selflessness that pushes others to the forefront before exalting myself. Our disaster relief efforts should be of the same selfless motive and heart.

Remember that full recovery requires a long-term commitment.

All too often, recovery efforts are forgotten when the media find something else to talk about. Everyone takes notice, responds with an initial outpouring of love, and then forgets all about the disaster within a few weeks. But recovery isn't usually complete that quickly.

When we commit to sending some form of support to a recovery effort, we should continue to follow up on that investment and see it through. The needs may change over time, and we should use wisdom (and prayer) to determine how we can continue to best respond until our task is fully complete.

HOW YOU CAN HELP

There are lots of ways to get involved. Many churches even go as far as creating a disaster relief ministry team. I live in Florida, where hurricanes and tropical storms are a regular occurrence, and my church has a plan in place for how we can respond in the community if we take a direct hit from a nasty storm. We even train people and certify them in disaster recovery so that everyone is prepared when the need arises.

Besides making sure that you have a good plan and proper training in place for your own church, you should consider working with other organizations at the local and global levels in order to be able to respond when and where your help is needed. Here are some ways to get involved:

- **Develop strong relationships with first responders.** Having good connections with area first-responder teams will give you the "inside access" to what the most important needs are. At the police or sheriff's department, ask what their biggest needs are right now (even during nonemergency times) and seek ways to meet those needs. You can also host special community events to recognize and honor local law enforcement. This is a great project for churches or small groups. Ask the fire department how you can partner with them to deliver community safety programs to the public, or take time to deliver meals to local fire stations. At the hospital, ask how members of your church can volunteer.

- **Build collaborative relationships with other churches and organizations.** When this is done ahead of time, the network for responding is already in place when disaster strikes unexpectedly.
- **Participate in community events.** It's important that your community sees you being active before disaster strikes. Your credibility will be much stronger, and people will know where to go when the need arises.
- **Connect with World Vision (WorldVision.org).** Give to the Disaster Response Fund (a great option for families, groups, and churches) or sponsor a child (another great option for families).
- **Connect with the Salvation Army (Disaster .SalvationArmyUSA.org).** Not only can you, your family, or your group give money, materials, or time to this ministry but you can also attend classes in the Salvation Army's disaster-training program so that you're prepared.
- **Connect with the Red Cross (RedCross.org).** A few ways you can get involved include giving blood or hosting a blood drive; taking, teaching, or hosting one of the Red Cross's offered classes; or becoming a digital advocate (raising money without having to donate).

The ability to respond to an emergency or disaster is about being ready. It's about being intentional. You can do things right now that will allow you to be a blessing to others when they are in a time of need. And just as important, you never know when you'll need to be a blessing to your own community. Taking steps now makes you prepared when the time comes and also gives you the opportunity to be a blessing to your community at this moment.

THINK IT THROUGH

Take a few minutes to digest what you've learned and answer the following questions. If you're reading this as a group, talk through your thoughts together.

1. In what ways have you been able to respond to disasters in the past? What worked well? Was there anything about the experience that made it difficult for you to connect with the cause? What would you do differently next time?
2. How ready are you (personally) for a disaster if one were to strike? What steps can you take right now to be better prepared?
3. What steps can you take right now to begin developing relationships with first responders and other community organizations?

HELPFUL TOOLS AND RESOURCES

For Research

- *Servolution: Starting a Church Revolution Through Serving*, by Dino Rizzo (Zondervan, 2009)
- *The Disaster Preparedness Handbook*, 2nd ed., by Dr. Arthur T. Bradley (Skyhorse Publishing, 2011)

For Action

- Go to SamaritansPurse.org for more ways to get involved.
- Check out WorldRelief.org for more ways to get involved.
- Join others in this movement and discussion at bibledude.net/activistfaith.

CHAPTER 6

HOME SWEET HOMELESS

BRINGING GOD'S SHELTER TO THOSE WHO NEED IT

Dillon Burroughs

> Sometimes it's easy to walk by because we know we can't change someone's whole life in a single afternoon. But what we fail to realize is that simple kindness can go a long way toward encouraging someone who is stuck in a desolate place.
>
> — Mike Yankoski, *Under the Overpass*

Noel Brewer Yeatts described a youth mission trip during which she and her friends met a five-year-old boy named Nildo, one of the many homeless street children of Brazil. Led to help him, her small mission team raised enough cash to purchase young Nildo new clothes and even helped finance a place for him at a local children's orphanage. Over the next year, Noel and her friends thought and spoke much of Nildo, wondering if he had remembered their efforts and time together.

When the next summer came, Noel's father arranged to take a trip to the same area. Before he left, Noel and her team prepared a Bible for Nildo that included a framed photo of those who had helped him the previous year. But the question remained: *Would Nildo still remember us?* Noel recounts her dad's story:

> Nildo hugged and kissed the photo and told everyone around him

> in loud Portuguese, "These are my American sisters! They took me off the streets."
>
> Later, my dad told us, "Girls, if you never do another good deed in your life, you have done something incredible for this one little boy."[1]

The elements of Noel's story are ones that can apply to the homeless plight of every person on the planet: a person in need, a person or group who identifies the need, a response, a life changed.

MY OWN STORY

In my early years, my family decided to build their own house and homestead on property in the Hoosier National Forest of southern Indiana. During the nine months of initial construction, our family of five survived in a two-person trailer without running water and only minimal electricity. We showered in an old tub with creek water and even used an outhouse for our restroom! At the age of eight, it felt like a long camping trip.

Years later, I would travel to developing nations and experience real poverty that made my summer of trailer living seem like extravagance. In 2006, I took my first visit to Gramothe, Haiti, a small mountain village in the high-mountain elevations above Port-au-Prince. Clean water itself was a luxury, as was any kind of roof to sleep under.

Still, hope remained. A Haitian pastor named Willem Charles had launched a church a few years earlier with a heart to help those in his poverty-stricken nation both spiritually and physically. When I visited, his church included a school with around six hundred students, almost all of whom were previously unschooled, existing in the hills as field workers or helping parents raise their siblings. Today Willem's efforts reach more than two thousand children on two campuses in some of the most remote areas of the Western Hemisphere's poorest nation.

Willem's organization, Mountain Top Ministries, is also working beyond the classroom to change lives. When I arrived, many students lived in shacks consisting of a few cinder blocks with a sheet of corrugated metal as a roof. Today many houses have been constructed, by both outside missionaries and local Christians seeking to help their neighbors.

In nearby Mission of Hope Haiti, I have encountered a similar experience on a much larger scale. After the 2010 epic earthquake that killed two hundred thousand people across the nation, tens of thousands lived in tent cities. Just two weeks following the devastation, a friend and I stood in front of Haiti's demolished capitol building and witnessed the vast numbers of survivors who had patched together tarps and sticks to survive. Reuben, a new friend I met during my time in Haiti, drove us through Cité Soleil, considered the poorest slum in Port-au-Prince, where thousands of men, women, and children stood in line for a bucket of water and other rations. Even Reuben was concerned for his safety, as he mentioned being carjacked in the area in the past. At the time, all I could do was pray, asking God to extend help to those in need and use me in any way possible.

Mission of Hope Haiti had served the nation for more than a decade and was one of the first organizations to respond following the quake. For weeks, they provided medical treatment, food, water, and tents to thousands of individuals affected by the disaster. But as I witnessed during the days I spent serving in their midst, longer-term solutions were required.

The most essential of these needs was housing. The people of Haiti could not live in tents long term with any sense of safety or security. A plan was made. Five hundred homes would be built on the organization's property, funded by donors and built by Haitians who would then own the homes in this new community. Soon the original plan was not large enough. Currently, 650 homes are in progress.

And one of my favorite parts? In 2011, Mission of Hope began a partnership with another organization to provide housing for 150 deaf and severely handicapped households in Cité Soleil. Those now living in a new home include JoJo. JoJo was born without legs and arms and has spent all his life in a wheelchair. But he has an unbelievable joy. My friend Reuben wrote that JoJo said,

> I believe God created me like this for a purpose. He gave me many talents. . . . I can paint, using my mouth to hold the paintbrush. God is using me as an instrument and I am proud to be used by him. And yes, it's true, I am handicapped . . . no legs and no arms, but I have love and joy of the Lord in my heart.[2]

Those we pray for and those we invest in are often deeply transformed by one change: a place to call home.

HERE AND NOW

Upon my return to the States, it was difficult to readjust. The two dollars I spent on a cup of coffee was the amount the average Haitian made in an entire day of work. The thirty-five dollars I spent for a meal out with my family was enough to support a student for a month. Every purchase was now physically painful. Each time I turned off my lamp at night, all I could think about was how blessed I was and how little I was doing to change the situation in Haiti.

As I prayed and processed my newfound understanding regarding the importance of housing, I found an article in my local newspaper that cited that there are four hundred homeless people in my town at any given time. Approximately one-fourth of these individuals are under the age of eighteen. I may not be called to move to another country to live or to fix the housing problems of the entire world, but my community has needs as well, and they are needs I can do something about.

One of my experiments included contacting the local Habitat for Humanity. Amazingly, they had filled all of their housing construction volunteer teams for the rest of the year, so I looked for others who were helping the homeless in my community. Soon I discovered the Chattanooga Community Kitchen. A hub of social services, the Community Kitchen serves food to those in need, provides housing and job services, and much more.

Like many Americans, my schedule was already full—very full. But when I asked Community Kitchen where they needed help, they mentioned the need for volunteers to serve breakfast, so I did. That meant waking up at 5:30 a.m. to get there on time, but every week for an entire summer, I scooped bowls of oatmeal and poured cups of coffee for many of my community's homeless citizens.

Some of the homeless remained distant, yet others became friends. Those who desired to move forward and receive help with housing and other needs stayed after breakfast and were given assistance. Many of these people are now off the streets.

I love hearing stories of lives changed from the work of the Community Kitchen. Here's a recent one:

> A family that had relied on us for shelter this winter now has their own apartment.
>
> A client recently came to Brother Ron in need of shoes. The bottoms of his shoes were practically nonexistent. A local church had recently done a shoe drive for us and this was the day that Brother Ron was giving away 60 pairs of new shoes.
>
> A former client that had at one time lived under a bridge recently graduated from Chattanooga State. He came by to show us his certificate where he had been named to the National Technical Honor Society.[3]

Our city was once known for having a long-established tent city where numerous homeless individuals lived together in community. Once this location was dismantled, many of those looking for help found their way through the doors of the Community Kitchen. Now they no longer live in tents. They have a place to call home.

I can't take much credit or really any credit for the changes. They were all God, but they were also the result of the efforts of many individuals working together for the common good.

HOW YOU CAN HELP

Like me, you may have a heart to help but don't know where to begin. I encourage you to start small. It was Mother Teresa who said, "Small actions done with great love will change the world." Maybe you know of someone who's about to lose his or her home. If you work in finance, offer to help with loan paperwork to create a reasonable monthly payment for keeping the home. Or consider raising money with a small group of friends to pay even one mortgage payment.

MSNBC reported in 2011 that American home foreclosures accounted for 28 percent of all home sales, nearly six times higher than what it would be in a healthy housing market.[4] Yes, this is depressing news. Some would even call it a depression.

But foreclosure is not always inevitable. We sometimes see family, friends, and neighbors struggle to keep their homes. What if we did something to help? A friend of mine once said, "What would our nation be like if every American helped another American out of homelessness?" I would add, "What would our nation be like if every American helped another American keep their home?" Those in need aren't always across the ocean or in the run-down parts of town; sometimes they're next door. As Jesus said, "Love your neighbor as yourself" (Mark 12:31, NIV). In some cases, this might include helping someone make a mortgage payment.

James 2:16-17 teaches this principle: "If one of you says to him, 'Go, I wish you well; keep warm and well fed,' but does nothing about his physical needs, what good is it? In the same way, faith by itself, if it is not accompanied by action, is dead" (NIV). One of the best defenses against homelessness is prevention. Help someone keep his home.

- **Make it personal.** During my last year of college, I had a conversation with a friend named Allan who had a problem: He had nowhere to live. He was a student but had to leave his dad's place and didn't have anywhere to stay. My roommate, Chad, and I told him he could have our couch and stay as long as he'd like.

  He did. Allan stayed almost the entire semester. During that time, we built a better friendship and encouraged one another. When he moved, I missed him and hoped his new place would work out. Three years later, I discovered he was graduating and moving to attend seminary. He ended up becoming a campus minister to students at the University of Notre Dame. His life has changed the lives of many others, complete with a wife and young child he is raising to live for God.

  My roommate and I can't take any credit for what happened in Allan's life. We do, however, get to enjoy how God is working through someone we helped. When we share what we have to help those struggling with housing issues, God often uses the experiences to transform us as well. The way I live is different because of Allan. The decisions I will make today have changed because of my times at the Community Kitchen with our city's poor and my trips to Haiti to minister to those living in tents.

  Your life can be changed too. The beauty of serving the housing needs of others, whether near to or far from where we live, is the eternal impact it makes on both their lives and ours. We cannot help others without being helped ourselves. Our lives become better as we seek to better the lives of others. Feel like you can't do much to solve homelessness? You're not alone. But when we all act, homelessness will change. It will change the lives of those who need a place to stay *and* it will change the lives of us who do have a place to call home. There's no place like home, both now and for eternity.

- **Partner with the experts.** You can look into local service providers who serve the needs of your community's homeless. A local rescue mission or Habitat for Humanity chapter is often a great place to start. Meet the volunteer coordinator and take the plunge. Do what it takes to meet those in need, develop a friendship, and view the face of homelessness in person.
- **Do what you can (not what you can't).** In my situation, my schedule allowed me to serve my local shelter for only the summer months. That was three months of volunteering that filled a need. Now I support my local homeless ministries as I am able financially and speak out on their behalf. I haven't built a home, but I am helping build momentum to reduce homelessness in my town.

  Maybe your thing is construction. If so, you need to get in on the building side of your area's needs. Maybe your skill is cooking. There is a place for you to serve the homeless in your area. If you're an organizer, organize. If you're a web designer, offer to design a free website for a local provider. This is similar to what the apostle Paul mentioned in Romans 12:6-8:

> We have different gifts, according to the grace given us. If a man's gift is prophesying, let him use it in proportion to his faith; if it is serving, let him serve; if it is teaching, let him teach; if it is encouraging, let him encourage; if it is contributing to the needs of others, let him give generously; if it is leadership, let him govern diligently; if it is showing mercy, let him do it cheerfully. (NIV)

Use your ability, whether it's on this list or not, and use it to help those in need. God has given us these abilities to show His love. Serving the needs of the homeless is a great way to express it.

Sometimes you just have to open the door. Last November, our area experienced uncommonly low winter temperatures that threatened the lives of our community's homeless. Those living under bridges or in cars would not be safe overnight. The local day center decided to open its doors, offering mattresses, pillows, and blankets to those who stayed there for the evening. For three months, between 150 and 190 men, women, and children slept on the day center's floor every night. The youngest was six weeks old; the oldest was seventy-nine.[5] Lives were changed and potentially saved by simply opening the door.

- **Sound the alarm.** When there is an emergency, we sound an alarm. Fire alarms warn of a fire. Tornado sirens ring to warn of pending disaster. Homelessness is a disaster. Once we realize the need, we are called to speak out about it. As Proverbs 31:8-9 instructs, "Speak up for those who cannot speak for themselves, for the rights of all who are destitute. Speak up and judge fairly; defend the rights of the poor and needy" (NIV).

  There are many ways to sound the alarm. The best way is to personally talk with others about the housing needs in your area. For example, it can begin with asking, "Did you know that in 2011 there were more than 14 million vacant properties and 3.5 million homeless people in America? Does this seem right to you?"

  In my case, a newspaper article mentioning the number of local homeless residents captured my attention. Writing, whether for print or online, can make a huge impact in changing attitudes toward homelessness where you live. You can write something for your church bulletin or newsletter, for a local newspaper or magazine, on social media such as Facebook, and even on bumper stickers. The important thing is to use a wide variety of ideas to spread (accurate) information that helps the homeless.

- **Commit long term.** No one can do everything; everyone can do something. If everyone does something for a long time, a lot will change. Mark Horvath wrote, "I'll never forget my first night. All of a sudden and without warning, I found myself homeless in Koreatown near downtown Los Angeles. I was sober, but I had no money, no place to go and no one I could call for help. I was officially homeless."[6] No one expects to be homeless, but many are. Whether due to addictions, mental health issues, lack of money, home foreclosure, or simply some hard times, homelessness happens to many who least expect it. As people of faith, we are called to do what we can to make a difference.

  I've not had the experience of living on the streets, but I did have the opportunity to volunteer in a place that serves breakfast to the homeless and poor of my community. Although the experience was for only the summer weeks, it has left a lasting mark on my life. Now when I see the homeless on the streets of my community, I wave, say hi, and even personally know some of those I pass. When I have something to give, I give it.

  Not long ago, I was in a conversation and mentioned something about "one of my homeless friends." I caught myself, realizing that until then homelessness had been only an idea; now it had become real people with real hurts. I had looked into their eyes, granted dignity, and built trust. As I have the opportunity, I do what I can to help, give, and advocate on behalf of my homeless friends. Why? Because that's what friends do.
- **Become a homeless church.** In my book *Undefending Christianity*, I spoke about a homeless woman my wife and I met whom I'll call Rebecca. We had a decent conversation, including some talk about spirituality. She was already connected with a local social worker and had a church home.

We ended up encouraging her the best we could but felt highly inadequate to provide help beyond the moment.

As I drove home that night, I couldn't help but wonder what it would look like had I invited Rebecca to my church that next morning. My church is great, but she would not have fit in there. Why? I rarely meet a homeless person attending our church. We're trying to help those in need and do better now than a few years ago, but our Sunday mornings are not designed with Rebecca in mind. Sound familiar?

Most churches are in similar situations. They want to help but don't know how to care for their local homeless while also serving the needs of current members. I encourage churches to become known as places where the poor and homeless can go to find help. If I came to your town and asked any person, "What church should I go to if I want to get involved in helping the poor of this community?" would your church be the first one mentioned? Make this your goal. Of course, this is not easy. If it were, every church would do it. In fact, you'll likely get in trouble along the way. In some cities, you must now obtain a permit to simply feed the homeless. For example, in Dallas, those who desire to distribute food must first become certified via a city-run food handlers' class. Denver has banned eating and sleeping on public property without permission.[7]

Some churches that have taken their local homeless residents seriously have garnered national attention, including being mentioned in *Rolling Stone* magazine.[8] Community Covenant Church is one of several churches in the Santa Barbara area participating in Safe Parking, a program that offers space for homeless residents living in their cars to park overnight. Twenty-three parking lots in Santa Barbara "house" 150 people in 113 vehicles each night. A local counseling center oversees the program, assigning each vehicle to a specific lot. The lots are generally open from 7 p.m. to 7 a.m.[9] A San Diego church that attempted a similar outreach, however, was cited with a permit violation, so be sure to look into local laws and regulations before undertaking a movement of public outreach.[10]

Another approach used by a growing number of congregations is Family Promise (FamilyPromise.org), previously called Interfaith Hospitality Network. Now with 171 affiliates in forty-one states, this organization focuses on connecting religious groups with the ability to safely provide temporary housing for local homeless residents, especially families. Here's how it typically works: In partnership with a local day center, hosting rotates weekly among the ten to thirteen host congregations in a network. In turn, each host congregation provides lodging, three meals daily, and hospitality to a homeless family. A congregation allows the family to stay overnight either at the church facility or in the home of a church member during this time. The local congregation provides volunteers to build friendships and hospitality while Family Promise works with families for longer-term solutions regarding jobs and housing. This solution might not work for every church, but it offers an example of how local congregations can partner together to address housing needs of local citizens.

My local Family Promise in Chattanooga is a wonderful example of this type of partnership in action. Since its start more than fourteen years ago, Family Promise has helped 650 families and 1,216 children transition to self-sufficiency. A total of fifty-one local congregations partner together to change the face of homelessness in our area.[11] The local church is becoming the answer for homelessness.

Yet despite the large number of partners represented, this accounts for only about 5 percent of the area's congregations.

> Imagine if 10 or 25 or even 50 percent of the community's churches participated? If even 25 percent of the churches in my town participated, it would cover every homeless person in my community. What would it take to say this in your town?

There are many methods already in use by individuals and churches across our nation. These stories often go unnoticed and untold, but they are quietly transforming the lives of countless individuals facing homelessness in our nation. What will the story of your church be in the days ahead? What will *your* story be regarding your impact on the lives of the homeless? Let today be the day you choose to get involved.

THINK IT THROUGH

Take a few minutes to digest what you've learned and answer the following questions. If you're reading this as a group, talk through your thoughts together.

1. How do people in your local community view homeless individuals? What services already operate in your area?
2. What is one step you can personally take this week to begin to help someone without a home or at risk of losing a home? Consider contacting a local agency to ask about ways you can volunteer or help.
3. What is your church, school, or workplace doing to serve the poor and homeless in your community? What ideas do you have for a new project or involvement in an existing project to make a greater impact?

HELPFUL TOOLS AND RESOURCES

For Research

- *Beyond Homelessness: Christian Faith in a Culture of Displacement*, by Steven Bouma-Prediger and Brian J. Walsh (Eerdmans, 2008)
- *Disrupting Homelessness: Alternative Christian Approaches*, by Laura Stivers (Augsburg Fortress, 2011)

For Action

- Go to bibledude.net/activistfaith to join others who are passionately working to end homelessness.

CHAPTER 7

THE LEAST OF THESE

DEFENDING THE UNBORN

Daniel Darling

You may choose to look the other way, but you can never say again that you did not know.

—William Wilberforce

For ten long years, Ben and Carmen endured the sting of infertility. Then one Christmas Eve, they got the news: Carmen was pregnant.

A few days later, they visited Carmen's doctor but were surprised at her lack of excitement. Twelve years earlier, Carmen had been diagnosed with multiple sclerosis. Pregnancy could carry serious risks for both the mother and the baby. The doctor calmly suggested that Carmen terminate her pregnancy.

Carmen and Ben were stunned by the doctor's rather cavalier attitude toward the baby in Carmen's womb. For them, it wasn't a complicated choice. Carmen would carry her baby despite the cost, and she told her husband, "I don't care what happens to me. If it has to come down to my life or the child's, I want you to save the baby. I'm having this baby."

Not only did Carmen survive the pregnancy but she gave birth to a beautiful, healthy baby girl named Michelle. And she beat the odds with MS, living to see Michelle reach her sixteenth birthday.

Today Michelle Pirraglia is a vibrant young Long Island journalist. In a touching tribute to her parents, she wrote for Patheos, "My mom was a woman of faith and common sense, along with a lot of courage. She was not afraid of the risks involved because she knew the life inside her was her child, not merely a clump of cells."[1]

Michelle is a rare survivor in a generation that, unfortunately, often chooses the convenient injustice of legal abortion.

PRO-LIFE: A BIBLICAL POSITION?

On January 22, 1973, the United States Supreme Court issued a legally dubious decision in *Roe v. Wade*, legalizing abortion. Since that decision, this issue has been one of the most controversial. Culture watchers credit this as the single moral issue giving rise to the modern conservative political movement, galvanized largely by millions of politically active evangelical Christians.

Evangelicals generally view abortion as a gross injustice, the wanton taking of innocent and vulnerable life. The theology of the pro-life movement is grounded in orthodox teachings of the Christian faith, based on three foundational presuppositions.

First is the unique personhood of the unborn child. Both the Old and New Testaments affirm the life of the unborn. King David wrote majestically about his own unique conception:

> You formed my inward parts; you knitted me together in my mother's womb. I praise you, for I am fearfully and wonderfully made. Wonderful are your works; my soul knows it very well. My frame was not hidden from you, when I was being made in secret, intricately woven in the depths of the earth. Your eyes saw my unformed substance; in your book were written, every one of them, the days that were formed for me, when as yet there was none of them. (Psalm 139:13-16, ESV)

Words such as *knitted together* and *intricately woven* clearly indicate that the "unformed substance" in the womb has intrinsic value to the Creator God. Old Testament Scriptures include several other accounts of God's high view of the fetus (see Genesis 25:22; Job 10:8-12; 31:13-15; Psalm 119:73; Hosea 12:2-3). Old Testament Law called for severe penalties for anyone who even accidentally wounded or killed an unborn child (see Exodus 21:22-25).

For those who affirm the Old Testament as part of the inspired Word of God, there is no ambiguity. Scholar James K. Hoffmeier, in his book *Abortion: A Christian Understanding and Response*, wrote, "Looking at Old Testament law from a proper cultural and historical context, it is evident that the life of the unborn is put on the same par as the person outside the womb."[2]

A theology of fetal personhood is affirmed in the New Testament, featured most prominently in the entrance of Jesus Christ into the world. Orthodox Christian faith affirms the conception of the Christ child in Mary by the Holy Spirit. Jesus "became flesh," wrote John in the opening chapter of his epic gospel. Matthew recorded that an angel of the Lord told Joseph that the unborn baby inside Mary was indeed the Christ (see Matthew 1:18-20). And a proper view of Christ (see Philippians 2:7; Hebrews 4:15) must consider Jesus to have experienced the full range of fetal development, from conception to child development to adult maturity. Clearly, the Incarnation narrative considers the unborn Jesus to be more than a soul-less fetus but rather deity in the flesh.

And there is the unique incident recorded in the gospel of Luke involving the unborn John in the womb of Elizabeth, Mary's cousin. As Mary shared the news of her own pregnancy, the baby leapt inside Elizabeth's womb (see 1:39-44).

The second foundational presupposition is the high value of human life. Genesis opens with a profound statement about this. The inspired writer Moses informs us that while God *spoke* the rest of creation into existence, He *formed* man in His image. In Genesis 2:7,

God granted man the unique breath of life. Created in the image of God, stamped with the imprint of the Trinity, man was created above the rest. Man became a living soul (see Genesis 1:26; 2:7).

Because each human soul was created in the image of God (see verses 27-29), the taking of life is viewed across Scripture not just as a crime against another but as an act of rebellion against the Creator Himself: "Whoever sheds the blood of man, by man shall his blood be shed, for God made man in his own image" (9:6, ESV). When Cain slew his brother in cold blood, God told him that the "voice" of Abel's blood "is crying to me from the ground" (4:10, ESV). Murder is the chief weapon of the Enemy, Satan, whom Jesus labeled a "murderer" (John 8:44), the rotten fruit of the fall of man (see James 1:15).

In perhaps the most powerful of the Bible's many prohibitions against murder, the Ten Commandments declares, "You shall not murder" (Exodus 20:13, ESV). This edict is informed by the very first commandment, which demands exclusive worship of Jehovah. A healthy view of human life flows from a proper view of God.

The third presupposition is the treasured place of children. In Scripture, the high view of life flows naturally to this third pillar of pro-life theology. Consider the words of Solomon:

> Behold, children are a heritage from the LORD, the fruit of the womb a reward. Like arrows in the hand of a warrior are the children of one's youth. Blessed is the man who fills his quiver with them! He shall not be put to shame when he speaks with his enemies in the gate. (Psalm 127:3-5, ESV)

The Scriptures were written among cultures where children were considered disposable. That idea was pushed aside, with each child seen as a gift from the heavenly Father. I've personally observed the ancient ruins of Caesarea Philippi and stood near the ragged precipice overlooking a canyon where children were tossed, sacrificed in vain to the fertility gods. At times, this pagan practice even crept into Israel's culture, provoking the wrath of God, spoken through the prophets (see 2 Kings 21:2-6; Jeremiah 7:30-34; 15:3-4; Ezekiel 16:20-21,36-38; 20:31).

And in the Gospels, we see Jesus teaching a high view of children, pointing to their innocent faith as a catalyst for building His kingdom (see Matthew 19:14).

The sanctity of human life is also firmly anchored in historic church orthodoxy. Consider the words of second-century church father Tertullian, often called "The Father of Western theology" and "The Father of Latin Christianity":

> It does not matter whether you take away a life that is born, or destroy one that is coming to the birth. In both instances, destruction is murder. . . . We may not destroy even the fetus in the womb, while as yet the human being derives blood from other parts of the body for its sustenance. To hinder a birth is merely a speedier man-killing; nor does it matter when you take away a life that is born, or destroy one that is coming to the birth. That is a man which is going to be one; you have the fruit already in its seed.[3]

A couple of hundred years later, Jerome, who translated the Bible from Greek and Hebrew into Latin, said abortion was "the murder of an unborn child,"[4] as did Augustine.[5]

Fast-forward to the Reformation and you read the bold words of John Calvin, who wrote in his *Commentary on the Pentateuch*,

> The fetus, though enclosed in the womb of its mother, is already a human being, and it is a most monstrous crime to rob it of the life, which it has not yet begun to enjoy. If it seems more horrible to kill a man in his own house than in a field, because a man's house is his place of most secure refuge, it ought surely to be deemed more atrocious to destroy a fetus in the womb before it has come to light.[6]

These are just a few quotes from among the volumes written by church leaders from the first century until the present. Clearly, protection for the unborn has been a consistent position throughout church history.

PRO-LIFE: A SCIENTIFIC POSITION?

Today there is a growing body of medical evidence that confirms the biblical and historic pro-life position. A recent study produced for the National Right to Life Committee found unique human characteristics of babies in the womb. Among them:

- Upon fertilization, all human chromosomes are present and unique human life begins.
- By day twenty-two, a heart begins to beat with a child's own blood.
- By the third week, a child's backbone, spinal column, and nervous system begin developing, and the liver, intestines, and kidneys take shape.
- By the fifth week, eyes, hands, and legs develop. By week eleven, the baby can fully grasp objects with the hand, and all the organs are functioning.
- By the fourth month, a baby is pumping twenty-five quarts of blood a day.
- By the twentieth week, the baby can recognize the mother's voice.[7]

Popular author and pastor Randy Alcorn, in an article titled "When Does Each Human Life Begin?" shares the testimony of leading medical and scientific professionals:[8]

- Dr. Alfred M. Bongioanni, professor of obstetrics, University of Pennsylvania: "I have learned from my earliest medical education that *human life begins at the time of conception.* I submit that human life is present throughout this entire sequence from conception to adulthood and any interruption at any point throughout this time constitutes a termination of human life."

- Dr. Jerome LeJeune, genetics professor at the University of Descartes in Paris (discoverer of the Down syndrome chromosome): "After fertilization has taken place a new human being has come into being. . . . This is no longer a matter of taste or opinion. *Each individual has a very neat beginning, at conception.*"
- Professor Micheline Matthews-Roth, Harvard University Medical School: "It is scientifically correct to say that *an individual human life begins at conception.*"
- Professor Hymie Gordon, Mayo Clinic: "By all the criteria of modern molecular biology, *life is present from the moment of conception.*"
- Dr. Watson A. Bowes, University of Colorado Medical School: "The beginning of a single human life is from a biological point of view a simple and straightforward matter—*the beginning is conception.*"
- Dr. Landrum Shettles, pioneer in sperm biology, fertility, and sterility; discoverer of male- and female-producing sperm: "I oppose abortion. I do so, first, because I accept what is biologically manifest—that *human life commences at the time of conception*—and, second, because I believe it is wrong to take innocent human life under any circumstances."

It quickly becomes obvious from the examination of fetal development and testimonies of scientists that science does in fact support the pro-life position.

WHAT IS THE ROLE OF THE CHURCH?

So if the biblical, traditional, and scientific data affirm the sanctity of human life, what should be the response of the church? Many evangelicals are rightly tired of the culture wars, yet the sanctity of human life is woven into the very fabric of our gospel. We must consider abortion to be not a political issue but an issue of social justice. Consider the sheer numbers concerning legal abortion in America:

- Between 1975 and 2010, more than fifty-two million elected abortions were performed. To put that number into perspective, tally up all the U.S. war casualties, from the Revolutionary War to the present conflicts in Iraq and Afghanistan, and multiply that by forty,[9] or imagine one-sixth of the current population of the United States.
- Twenty-two percent of all pregnancies in America end in abortion.[10]

Confronted by the sheer numbers, many wonder, *What can we do?*

LIVING ON THE GRACE SIDE

When it comes to pro-life advocacy, Christians must increasingly speak with compassion and grace. The decision to keep a baby or to abort it involves real people and personal decisions. Often, calloused statements have tainted the pro-life cause as being "anti-women." We must defend the unborn, but not at the expense of demonizing those who disagree with us.

The Scriptures remind us that abortion is merely a symptom of a deeper human condition. Sin is the sickness that infects every human heart. Its fruit, James 1:15 reminds us, is death. But if sin is the problem, recognition of sin is the gateway to the cure, and not just for abortion but for every social ill. Adam's tragic moment in the garden didn't surprise God and neither does the injustice of abortion. The entrance of sin into the world triggered God's eternal plan of rescue, fulfilled in the birth, life, and death of Jesus Christ (see Romans 5:18-21).

So if the church lives on the grace side of abortion and other social sins, it should be in the church where the victims of sin's devastation find the transformative power of the gospel and where the redeemed work with God to restore justice to a fallen world.

Abortion is a tragic sin against a holy God, but it is no match for the depth and width of God's grace. For the millions who have made the choice to end a life, there is a river of forgiveness available that flows from Immanuel's veins. Hymn writer William Cowper powerfully stated, "Sinners plunge beneath that flood, lose all their guilty stains."[11]

Because God's redeemed people have personally experienced this grace and carry this message, the church, more than any other institution in society, is uniquely positioned to bring hope for overcoming the tragedy of abortion.

PRO-LIFE ACTIVISM IN THE TWENTY-FIRST CENTURY

The Bible calls us to live on the side of grace, not merely cursing the darkness of abortion and those who practice it but working to offer solutions in saving lives, both physically and eternally, one soul at a time.

The church has a variety of tools in its arsenal for promoting a culture of life.

Gospel-Centric Preaching

It was British prime minister Margaret Thatcher who was fond of saying, "First you win the argument, then you win the vote." The most effective pro-life message is the gospel itself, the countercultural idea that man has unique human dignity and worth and is the object of

God's special love and of Jesus' personal sacrifice. The gospel, consistently and compassionately delivered, has the power to permeate all corners of society, including the very sensitive issue of abortion. By its nature, it creates advocates for life.

Pastor Jared Wilson agrees, writing thoughtfully on his blog *The Gospel-Driven Church*,

> Here's the thing: Pastors who preach culture war receive Amens from the already convinced and almost nothing from everybody else. At its worst, a steady dose of this creates an unhealthy "us vs. them" mentality that has us thinking of our enemies in ways the Sermon on the Mount strictly forbids. But pastors who proclaim the freedom from sin and abundant life in Christ lay groundwork for zeal for life, not just for winning political battles. A gospel-driven pro-life agenda means hating abortion *because we love women and we love the unborn.* That sounds like a no-brainer but so many of our evangelical countrymen just sound like they hate abortion. And preaching isn't just for pastors. In general, more evangelicals need to talk Jesus more than they talk politics. . . . Let's return to the good news of the kingdom of God.[12]

Effective Cultural Argument

Christians must also make winsome, grace-filled cultural arguments, and we can be encouraged by the increasing support for the pro-life cause in the public at large. A 2012 Gallup poll found that only 41 percent of Americans were pro-choice, a record low in the history of the poll.[13] Gallup also discovered younger generations of Americans to be more pro-life than their parents. College students, not typically known as champions of conservatism, were also increasingly engaging the pro-life cause.[14] A 2013 conference of Students for Life of America sold out for the fifth year in a row with more than two thousand attendees.[15] And there is a rising generation of pro-life advocacy among women. In 2003, the Center for the

Advancement of Women, a pro-choice organization, found that a majority of women believe that abortion should be legally prohibited.[16]

I believe this is the fruit of effective gospel preaching and evangelism as well as powerful and creative cultural arguments. One organization, Heroic Media, runs thirty-second commercials over a course of ten weeks in selected markets, educating the public about the sanctity of life and advertising the services of a free crisis helpline. Heroic Media has found a 20 percent reduction in the abortion rate in the markets where their commercials are broadcast.[17]

There is even a subtle shift in pop-culture offerings. In recent years, episodes of *Law and Order* and *House* have given a compassionate pro-life message, depicting the agony of abortion and portraying the pro-life message in a positive light. Even MTV's recent abortion special *No Easy Decision*, though supportive of abortion, nevertheless portrayed the regret of one young woman who chose to end her pregnancy.

Matt Lewis, columnist for *The Daily Caller*, sees momentum, writing,

> Much of the same Christian ethos that led to great social causes like the abolition movement are alive and well within the modern pro-life movement. In fact, just as many abolitionists were Christians who viewed slavery as a moral issue, many pro-lifers feel the same way. . . . Many pro-lifers (I am one) believe we will one day look back on this point in history—when abortions are legal and not terribly rare—with the same level of amazement, sadness, and deep regret that we now feel when we look back on the days of slavery.[18]

Perhaps one day we'll look back on the practice of abortion and consider it the tragic relic of an unsophisticated society. Maybe it will occupy the same place in our history as slavery, Jim Crow laws, and other past injustices.

Local Pro-Life Ministry

The unsung heroes in the fight for the unborn may not be the politicians or the preachers but rather the nearly forty thousand volunteers around the country who work tirelessly with young unwed mothers. I've worked with a few of these volunteers in our local community and have been impressed by their heart for the welfare of the young women who come into their care.

According to a recent survey conducted by a consortium of national pro-life organizations, it is estimated that perhaps ninety thousand lives have been saved by the nearly twenty-three thousand crisis pregnancy clinics across America. Most offer ultrasounds to clients, which is highly effective, as an estimated 60 percent of women who view an ultrasound choose life. These clinics not only walk women through their various options but also offer parenting support and training, free resources such as diapers and food, and even post-abortive counseling. According to a recent survey of post-abortive women, seven out of ten said that if they had been given the opportunity to review their options, they would have chosen life.

Incredibly, the vast majority of crisis pregnancy centers run on a shoestring budget. Most are staffed by volunteers and funded by local churches. They see an estimated two million women every year, with each center averaging about 350 to 400 women. Despite being largely understaffed and underfunded (twenty-nine out of every thirty workers is a volunteer), they serve on the front lines, rescuing people from the edge of death.[19]

In her book *Blue Like Play Dough*, Tricia Goyer shared how her own experience as an unwed mother motivated her to become a powerful advocate for unwed teenage girls. In her hometown in Montana, she led the effort in her church to begin a crisis pregnancy center. It began as one room, supplied by the meager donations of church members and churches in the area, who donated used clothes, baby toys, and essentials such as diapers, formula, and wipes. The center ran a few advertisements in the local newspaper and on the radio.

They were surprised at how many young girls began to knock on the church door. In one year, they found the abortion rate in their town had reduced by one-third.[20]

There are millions of women and young girls who live in our neighborhoods who find themselves pregnant and alone. Their families might have rejected them, the boyfriend escaping in fear. They face the mountain of motherhood alone and wonder how or if they can raise a child on their own.

This is where the church is uniquely positioned to respond with the gospel, lived out with the grace of compassion. Imagine if conservative Christians invested less in political-action committees, candidates, and partisan media and instead opened their wallets and supported crisis pregnancy centers? What if we doubled and tripled the number of clinics around the country? And what if we invested in long-term counseling and support for mothers who decided to keep their babies? The power is in our hands to give mothers the information and resources they need.

Political Influence

While many younger evangelicals, such as myself, have grown weary of decades of seemingly fruitless political activity, we must not give up on the effort to legally protect the unborn.

Pro-life advocates in state legislatures and in Congress have worked hard to pass pro-life laws that work to curb abortions. And although we have not yet seen a national ban on abortion, legislation at the state level has been successful in reducing the number of abortions.[21] This is important work. Every generation needs winsome, faithful Christians committed to stand for life in the political arena, and we need people of faith to support those who run. As we engage in the political process, however, and as we maintain a Christlike spirit in the midst of a contentious national debate, we must be discerning, pragmatic, and wise, avoiding the temptation to view one party, election, or dynamic personality as the ultimate solution.

Expanding the Pro-Life Portfolio

New generations of evangelical activists are expanding the pro-life portfolio to include other issues of injustice. To affirm the human dignity of every soul is to be concerned about the plight of children around the world, many who suffer from poor nutrition or lack of other basic needs. It is to act on behalf of AIDS victims, stand strongly against human trafficking, and adopt a more biblically nuanced view of immigration and refugees.

Pro-life activism can also affirm the dignity of human life by addressing the problems of fatherlessness and at-risk children in our communities. Organizations such as Boys & Girls Clubs, Donald Miller's The Mentoring Project, Tony Dungy's work with All Pro Dad, and Robert Lewis's Men's Fraternity serve to connect responsible men with young children in need of important role models.

These organizations are doing wonderful things, and every church is also equipped to support young families and fill the gaps so single parents can effectively raise children. Churches must provide spiritual support, which helps eliminate risk factors that contribute to the tragic choices leading to abortion.

THE EASY WAY OUT

A well-rounded, biblical pro-life perspective meets the injustice of the age with the grace of the gospel. If the anger that rises from the injustice of abortion only fuels us to tune into another talk-radio program or forward another snarky political e-mail or add another in-your-face badge to our Facebook pages, we've failed the unborn who await our rescue. If we're really passionate about the pro-life issue, it should drive us to be the solution in our local communities. We might not have the power to overturn *Roe v. Wade*, but can we introduce a mother to real Life through her Savior? Can we save a baby from the precipice of death, one life at a time?

Consider the example of the midwives in Exodus. They served

under a pharaoh who ordered the murder of innocent Jewish boys. It was an unjust policy they were powerless to overturn, but that didn't stop them from saving the babies in front of them, the lives they had the opportunity to spare. The sheer magnitude of the crisis didn't deter them from being the solution.

The church can meet sin with the grace of Calvary's Cross. When a teenage girl gets pregnant, she often feels unworthy, alone, and ashamed. Will the church welcome her into its midst even though an unwed mother represents a violation of God's sacred purpose for sex? Can we affirm her value as a beloved child of the Creator as well as the value of sexual purity while recognizing the fallen nature of our world? Can we demonstrate love to the mother and her child without affirming her actions?

Scripture reminds us that the young mother is not our real enemy. Neither is the pro-choice politician or even the abortionist. The sin of abortion is the work of our real enemy, Satan. We don't fight flesh and blood; we fight principalities and powers, spiritual wickedness in high places (see Ephesians 6:12).

HOW YOU CAN HELP

It seems impossible to save the millions of babies aborted each year. But while you may not be able to overturn *Roe v. Wade* by yourself, you can actually save the life of an unborn child in your community. Here are some ways you can live out your pro-life values on the local level:

- **Assist or establish a local crisis center.** Are you aware of a local crisis pregnancy center in your area? If not, you might check the Care Net website (Care-Net.org) and find one nearby. If there is a local one, I encourage you to walk in and ask if there is any way you can volunteer your time. You might also ask if your church can help partner to raise money for the center through a "baby bottle" campaign, in which donors give a bottle filled with loose coins, cash, or checks. If you don't have a center in your local area, prayerfully consider spearheading an effort to start one. You might begin by speaking with the leaders in your local church and other churches and pro-life organizations. One way to involve your whole family would be to organize a supply drive for items such as baby clothes, formula, diapers, and maternity clothes.

- **Establish an outreach to young single moms at your church.** Teen moms need support and care and are often very open to parenting help. You might consider launching a Teen MOPS chapter or something like it that offers counseling and support. Check out Tricia Goyer's website (TriciaGoyer.com) for more information.
- **Support education efforts.** You might consider supporting organizations such as Heroic Media (HeroicMedia.org) or Focus on the Family's CitizenLink (CitizenLink.com). Both organizations offer smart, compassionate media efforts to educate the public on the issue of abortion.
- **Support local legislative efforts.** The real momentum in codifying protections for the unborn into law seems to be on the state level. Organizations such as the National Right to Life federation or local right-to-life groups are great resources to follow on pending legislation. A word of wisdom, however: Be careful to maintain a Christian testimony in winsomely engaging the fight, even when you disagree. Legislators need to hear your views on this issue, and you should use this as a calculus for determining your vote.
- **Support your local church's efforts.** Be pro-life where you can in your local church. Support families and children and parenting ministries. Affirm the value of life by your time and your witness.

The only hope for the abortion crisis is the gospel message, lived out daily by those who have witnessed its transforming power.

It's easy to forget our own fallenness and redemption when we get wrapped up in the what and how of the matter instead of the why. We see the abortionist who stands at the foot of the cross, blood on his hands. Next to him stands the woman who chose to end the life within her womb. But next to them stands the husband with the secret addiction, the self-righteous church gossip, and the pastor with his own checkered past, each a recipient of God's unmatched grace.

Followers of Christ have a choice: curse the darkness or join with Christ in rescuing and restoring life.

THINK IT THROUGH

Take a few minutes to digest what you've learned and answer the following questions. If you're reading this as a group, talk through your thoughts together.

1. How can you be sure that abortion is wrong according to the Bible?
2. Why is this more than a political issue?
3. What steps can you take now in your local community to help save babies at risk and support young mothers?

HELPFUL TOOLS AND RESOURCES

For Research

- *Blue Like Play Dough*, by Tricia Goyer (Multnomah, 2009)
- *ProLife Answers to ProChoice Arguments*, by Randy Alcorn (Multnomah, 2000)
- "5 Easy Ways to Be ProLife," ActivistFaith.org

- Randy Alcorn, "When Does Each Human Life Begin? The Answer of Scripture," http://www.epm.org/resources/2010/Jan/29/when-does-each-human-life-begin-answer-scripture/
- Trevin Wax, "Roe v. Wade at 37," http://thegospelcoalition.org/blogs/trevinwax/2010/01/18/roe-v-wade-at-37/
- A Passion to Serve (APassiontoServe.org), to read about the incredible effectiveness of pregnancy centers in reducing the number of abortions

For Action

- Care-Net.org has a nationwide directory of crisis clinics and information about how you can establish one in your community.
- Option Ultrasound (ministry of Focus on the Family) helps equip pregnancy centers with ultrasound machines (http://www.heartlink.org/oupdirectors.cfm).
- Go to bibledude.net/activistfaith to join others in the pro-life movement.

CHAPTER 8

WAR, TERROR, AND GENOCIDE

THREE GOLIATHS FOR CHRISTIAN ACTION

Dan King

> You have heard that it was said, "Love your neighbor and hate your enemy." But I tell you: Love your enemies and pray for those who persecute you.
>
> — Jesus (Matthew 5:43-44, NIV)

Can you imagine giving up everything? Walking away from your family, friends, and entire way of life? Jumping ship from Islam and converting to Christianity means that you're walking away from all of this and probably inviting your own death sentence. That's because many extreme Islamists believe that death is the only way out of the religion.

That's what Mosab Hassan Yousef, the son of one of the founding members of Hamas, did when he abandoned his Muslim faith and denounced his father's organization. Hamas (an acronym for the phrase that is translated as "Islamic Resistance Movement") is classified as a terrorist organization in the United States, Canada, the European Union, and several other countries. Their goal is to do away with Israel and the Palestinian Territories and replace them with a new Islamic Palestinian state. The methods they've used to accomplish those goals include rocket attacks and suicide bombings.

Yousef was arrested and jailed by Israel at age ten for throwing rocks at Israeli settlers. Since then, he's been detained numerous times in Israeli prisons for crimes against Israeli citizens. During one particular three-month prison stay, he witnessed several acts of violence by Islamic Hamas members against other Islamic Hamas members. It was then that he started to realize there are some problems with the organization's core beliefs. The seed had been planted for him to begin questioning his upbringing and Muslim faith.

Not long after that experience, he met a British missionary in a random encounter on the streets of Jerusalem. The missionary invited him to read parts of the Christian Bible with him, and because Yousef was curious about other perspectives and worldviews, he accepted the offer. It was during this time when he read something that shook him to his core. It was one of the teachings of Jesus in the gospel of Matthew. Three simple words stood out: "Love your enemies." The concept was completely foreign to the views he had been taught—to hate and destroy your enemies—and those three words caused him to completely reexamine everything.

Yousef studied the religious texts from both faith systems. In the Christian Bible, he found what he believed to be the actual words of God. In the Koran, he found inconsistencies and self-serving doctrine. Today he is an evangelical Christian living under political asylum in the United States. His goal is to inspire a new generation of youth (future leaders) with the truth about a Muslim faith that has a tendency toward violence rather than love. It's definitely a noble cause, and it cost him everything. In doing this, he walked away from power (as a future star in the Hamas party) and family (who disowned him after his decision).

And as much as Yousef would like to see peace, especially in the Middle East, he recognizes that it's not likely. As long as there are people who are hungry for power, there will be war. And in the case of militant Muslim organizations such as Hamas, these people will use religious texts, such as the Koran, to justify their position and rally people into the fight with them.[1]

THE QUESTION OF WAR

It seems like the best way to start this conversation is to think through whether war is justified. It's not my intent to take a particular stand for or against war; rather, I hope to think through the reality of war in our world and build a foundation for how Christians should respond to the issues of war, terrorism, and genocide. The reality is that we live in a fallen and broken world, and wherever there are people who have different ideas and motivations, there will be conflict.

About 1,600 years ago, Saint Augustine had to deal with the realities that came along with the collapse of the Roman Empire. Prior to its collapse, in the hundred years following the conversion of Constantine, the church was under the protection of the state. When that protection no longer existed, Christians were forced to evaluate their response to this question: If an oppressive government replaced the Roman Empire, would they fight to maintain their right to worship God?

In answer to the question, Augustine developed his doctrine of military ethics, commonly referred to today as Just War Theory. There are two sets of criteria that he developed related to defining "just war": *jus ad bellum* (the right to go to war) and *jus in bello* (right conduct in war).[2]

Jus ad bellum deals with defining why a country can and should go to war in the first place. The idea is to prevent people and leaders from pursuing self-serving purposes and using the military as pawns in their power struggles. The elements of *jus ad bellum* are as follows:

- **Just cause.** This involves such things as the protection of innocent life and preventing severe injustice against human rights.
- **Comparative justice.** The idea here is that in a conflict, when

one party is suffering far greater than the other, war may be justified to protect the oppressed.

- **Competent authority.** This criterion states that only political authorities within systems that allow distinctions of justice are authorized to declare war. This rules out dictatorships and rogue military leaders.
- **Right intention.** The intention of entering into war can be only to correct wrongs, not for material gain.
- **Probability of success.** There must be a chance of winning. War must not be entered into if there is no chance of coming out on top. The loss of life just for the sake of entering war is not justifiable.
- **Last resort.** Peaceful options must be pursued first, and all alternatives must be exhausted before using force.
- **Proportionality.** The benefits of entering into war must be proportionate to the expected harm caused by that war.

Once a conflict has begun, *jus in bello* tells us how war must be conducted. Just as important as having rules for ethically entering into war, having guidelines for conduct during war prevents us from performing the very kinds of injustices we're trying to counteract. The elements of *jus in bello* are as follows:

- **Distinction.** The acts of war should be directed at combatants who are engaged in the battle. Civilian bystanders are innocent victims, and even combatants who have surrendered should be protected in order to prevent meaningless death.
- **Proportionality.** Attacks should not be excessive compared to what is required for anticipated military needs.
- **Military necessity.** Attacks should be only on military objectives and only as needed to accomplish military objectives.

- **Fair treatment of prisoners of war.** Respect for all human life should override military objectives when combatants no longer pose a threat.
- **No means *malum in se*.** Weapons and tactics considered evil or excessive should not be used.

There are several nonviolent sects of Christianity who believe that all war is wrong; others feel that it may be justified in certain situations. It can be difficult to take a stand either way. Jesus was outspoken against violence with His "Put away your sword" and "Turn the other cheek" statements. And His message of love stands strong in the face of any sort of violent activity. But even hard-line nonviolence activists must admit that it's difficult to stand by while other people suffer horrible injustices at the hands of tyrants.

Even with criteria like the ones outlined by Saint Augustine, it can be somewhat easy for manipulative leaders to twist the truth in order to justify war. That's what makes it difficult to determine whether a given war is acceptable or not.

Regardless of whether you agree with war, it's easy to see how Augustine's criteria for just war provide a baseline for ethical conduct when conflict does exist. In fact, some of the biggest injustices we can think of happen when these guidelines are ignored. That's where acts of terrorism and genocide stem from.

Terrorism, as experienced during the 9/11 attacks on the World Trade Center, usually violates several of the criteria of Augustine's *jus ad bellum* and *jus in bello*. Likewise, genocide violates Augustine's criteria quite substantially. Genocide can be described as "the deliberate and systematic destruction, in whole or in part, of an ethnic, racial, religious, or national group."[3] One of the largest and most well-known acts of genocide is the genocidal policy of Nazi Germany that claimed the lives of somewhere around six million Jews and more than ten million Slavs.[4] More recently, the Rwandan Genocide in 1994 stands out, as the Hutu people conducted mass killings of approximately

800,000 Tutsi people (about 20 percent of the nation's total population) as a result of fear stemming from ethnic tension and power struggles between the two groups.

When you think about acts of extreme evil and injustice, it's a little easier to see where force may be the only option to protect human life. But in Christian circles, the use of force still carries a certain stigma. For example, one of the criticisms I observed of the Kony 2012 campaign in Uganda was that it seemed to encourage military action. This was especially tricky because much of Joseph Kony's Lord's Resistance Army (LRA) consists of child soldiers abducted and forced to fight on his behalf. It's difficult to argue that killing children, even when they are the combatants, is justified.

Whether you agree with using war or force to intervene in a "justifiable" situation, the impacts of war go far beyond the ethical dilemma. Wartime situations put people in extreme circumstances that result in other needs that the church can be instrumental in addressing.

VICTIMS OF WAR

Unfortunately, there are rarely any winners in war. There's nothing glamorous about it, and people die. Even those who survive often carry the weight of the war with them for a long time. The impacts may vary quite a bit, but the pain of war is a reality that many deal with. Healing and restoration is needed by everyone involved. I believe that those affected the most by war fall into three categories:

- Noncombatant victims of unjust acts of war, terrorism, and genocide
- Soldiers and veterans (even those in a "just war" scenario)
- Family members of soldiers who are fighting in a war

As you can imagine, each of these groups has different kinds of issues that need to be dealt with, and that means there's room in each of these areas for the church to minister. Because the issues are very different, how we deal with them may also look very different. And it doesn't matter whether we agree with the specific act of war or even war in general. What matters is that as Christians we are called to bring healing to the sick and restoration and hope to the world. So wherever there are people who are hurting, there the church should be ministering to those needs.

Noncombatant Victims

This category is probably the most tragic of the three. These are the innocent victims who just happened to be in the way of violence. The terrible thing is that they aren't even part of the fight. And although some of these casualties could be accidental, it's most likely that they were intentional, especially in the case of terrorism and genocide.

When you begin to count the casualties, it also becomes clear that those who die aren't the only victims. Survivors are the ones who never asked to be part of a wartime situation but still suffer the physical, emotional, and often spiritual damage that was inflicted upon them.

The emotional wounds these victims suffer may be some of the most difficult to overcome simply because of the often-unexpected nature of the attack. Where soldiers, and even their families, expect the possibility of injury or death, noncombatant casualties are pulled in against their will. This can result in more questions of why. Some estimates I've read over the years have stated that the incidence of post-traumatic stress disorder (PTSD) for innocent victims is substantially higher than even veterans of the Vietnam War.

Soldiers and Veterans

This group of victims is probably the most obvious. While these people are most likely much more aware of the impacts of the wartime action they're exposed to, few are ever fully prepared mentally and spiritually for the things they encounter and witness. When you strap on a rifle and willingly walk into a war zone, you have an eyes-wide-open understanding of what could happen. However, one thing that military training cannot replicate is the actual experience of casualties that will inevitably occur.

I've served in the U.S. Marine Corps and have experienced the training that every Marine must go through in order to be battle ready. We spent a great deal of time on the rifle range learning how to fire our weapons accurately. I can completely disassemble an M-16 and put it back together in a matter of seconds—with my eyes closed. And I can demonstrate the proper way to attach a bayonet to the end of my rifle and use it on a stuffed dummy. But I cannot tell you what it's like to take a bullet or get stabbed with a bayonet myself.

I'm fortunate that I never saw actual battle during my time in the military, though I have many friends and family who have. And they can tell you all about the horrible feelings they've struggled with as a result of either being injured themselves or witnessing a close friend get injured or even die next to them. Even when you expect that it can happen, being a part of that can really mess with your head. It's these struggles that lead to alcoholism, drug use, and divorce among wartime veterans. I also suspect it is these kinds of issues that lead many veterans of war to not be able to cope in normal society as effectively as the rest of us, resulting in higher rates of homelessness. It's a shame when one of the largest demographics of homeless people consists of veterans, the people who fought for our freedom.

Family Members of Soldiers

Another "innocent bystander" group affected by war is the family, particularly the spouses and children, of soldiers serving in a war. The impact on families is obvious when you watch some of the viral videos on the Web of soldiers returning home and surprising their loved ones with their arrival. Children who stay strong for months on end while Daddy is away at war break down completely when they see him show up safe at home. This kind of joy is a clear sign of how deep the emotional impact is, even though they appear to be strong and have it all together while he's gone.

Families who have someone away at war need support at a couple of different levels. First, when the soldier is away, these families must function as they normally do with only one spouse there to manage everything. Maintaining a family as a single parent is never easy, especially when you throw in the added stress of not knowing if you'll ever hear from the other spouse again. The time when one spouse is away at war can be one of the most difficult experiences some families ever go through. Churches that provide military families with additional support (material, spiritual, and emotional) can make a big difference in the family's ability to get through a tough time.

Second, additional support may be needed when a family member is lost in war. Typically, the military will provide certain survivor benefits to families, but these benefits will typically be more financial (such as life insurance) than anything else. Losing a spouse (or parent, if you are a child) can alter a person's life drastically. Having a support structure in place for these people can help them work through the trauma and emotional or spiritual impacts they are likely to experience.

DEALING WITH THE IMPACTS OF WAR

You don't have to be a soldier engaged in an act of war to suffer from PTSD. There are many victims in war, and each one needs the compassionate healing power of Christ that the church can offer if we look past political agendas and see all of these victims for who they are: people in need of healing and restoration.

PTSD can result in a variety of issues that survivors may deal with for long periods of time. Sufferers of PTSD often relive the traumatic event in their minds, revert to avoidance, and experience increased anxiety, anger, and guilt. Often victims turn to substance abuse as a coping mechanism, and in extreme cases, they may struggle with suicidal tendencies. These are deep emotional scars that take a long time and a great deal of effort to heal. Many who suffer PTSD require a great deal of counseling and spiritual healing.

Even the Department of Veterans Affairs (VA) recognizes the importance of spirituality in healing from PTSD:

> Aspects of spirituality are associated with positive outcomes, even when trauma survivors develop psychiatric difficulties such as PTSD or depression. Research also indicates that healthy spirituality is often associated with lower levels of symptoms and clinical problems in some trauma populations. For example, anger, rage, and a desire for revenge following trauma may be tempered by forgiveness, spiritual beliefs, or spiritual practices.[5]

The VA identifies four things that a good spiritual foundation does in helping PTSD victims recover from the trauma:

1. **Reduces behavioral risks through healthy religious lifestyles.** When people fill their lives with positive activities and spiritual disciplines such as reading the Bible, worship, prayer, and serving other people through ministry and outreach, they are less likely to fill that void with unhealthy coping mechanisms. These uplifting, faith-based activities help the PTSD victim maintain a positive focus on the things that are good about life.
2. **Expands social support through involvement in spiritual communities.** One of my favorite things about church is that it feels like family. In fact, sometimes it feels more like family than biological family. This kind of spiritual community is available and eager to bring you a meal when you're having a rough day, watch the kids to give you some time out, be a friendly shoulder to cry on, and intercede in prayer on your behalf. This kind of community can lay a strong foundation for the road to recovery and healing for victims.

3. **Enhances coping skills and helps victims better understand the trauma.** While traumatic events can often cause people to question God and His intentions (and some may believe that no good can come from their loss or trauma), having a faith system can help people find meaning for the events. By connecting personal experiences to the greater purpose God gives us in life, victims are often able to come to peace with the events.
4. **Develops physiological mechanisms, such as activation of the "relaxation response," through prayer or meditation.** The physical benefits of prayer have been proven scientifically through many different studies. In addition to the spiritual benefit of talking to God through regular times of prayer, studies have shown that it reduces stress levels and can result in a relaxed state. For someone who is dealing with stress-related disorders, this has obvious positive effects.

HOW YOU CAN HELP

One thing that drives me crazy is when people think that antiwar protests are the kind of activism that Jesus called the church to. I can tell you that even though I've served in the military, I'm not a big advocate of war, but I recognize that not everyone is going to believe the same thing that I do. Simply trying to tell others why they're wrong isn't going to change much of anything. However, the one thing that can make a difference is the one thing that rocked Mosab Hassan Yousef's world: "Love your enemies."

The most important factor in guiding the Christian response in matters of war, terrorism, and genocide is to determine whether what we're doing is motivated by love, healing, and reconciliation. For starters, here is a list of things you can do today to respond with love:

- **Adopt a Terrorist for Prayer (ATFP.org).** Adopt a terrorist and commit to praying for that individual. You might choose to do this as a family or a small group and pray together daily or weekly.
- **Help wounded warriors and support local troops.** Military Ministry of Campus Crusade for Christ (MilitaryMinistry.org) has a "Bridges to Healing" program. You can register your church to conduct Military Marriage seminars.
- **Get resources to share with wives/families of deployed soldiers.** Faith Deployed (FaithDeployed.com) has speakers available to visit your church, group, or ministry.
- **Financially support wounded warriors in need of care.** You can donate frequent flyer miles through Air Compassion for Veterans (AirCompassionforVeterans.org) to get wounded warriors to the medical treatment facilities they need.

Through an outpouring of Christian love to all types of victims of war, terrorism, and genocide, the church can leave an unmistakable mark on this world. And who knows? Maybe if we continue to pour out the kind of love and healing that only the church is capable of, we can create a world where war is not how we deal with each other. I believe that love can change things.

THINK IT THROUGH

Take a few minutes to digest what you've learned and answer the following questions. If you're reading this as a group, talk through your thoughts together.

1. How can you actively love your enemy today? Who is your enemy, and how can you bless him or her?
2. Is there a military base nearby? How can you connect with the

chaplains to find out what their greatest needs are and how you or your church can meet those needs?

3. How can you be a blessing to spouses of active-duty military stationed overseas?
4. Check with your local military recruiters and VA offices to see if there are things you can do for those entering or returning from military service. What needs can you meet?

HELPFUL TOOLS AND RESOURCES

For Research

- *War, Peace, and Christianity*, by Timothy J. Demy and J. Daryl Charles (Crossway, 2010)
- *Son of Hamas: A Gripping Account of Terror, Betrayal, Political Intrigue, and Unthinkable Choices*, by Mosab Hassan Yousef (Tyndale, 2011)
- *Two Wars: One Hero's Fight on Two Fronts—Abroad and Within*, by Nate Self (Tyndale, 2009)

For Action

- Go to OperationBandanas.org and CombatFaith.com for more opportunities to serve.
- Visit bibledude.net/activistfaith to partner with others who are passionately seeking ways to make a difference in a war-torn world.

CHAPTER 9

WHY I AM ILLEGAL IN MORE THAN FIFTY COUNTRIES

STANDING FOR RELIGIOUS FREEDOM HERE AND EVERYWHERE

Dillon Burroughs

> Remember those in prison as if you were their fellow prisoners, and those who are mistreated as if you yourselves were suffering.
>
> — Hebrews 13:3 (NIV)

I am illegal in more than fifty countries.

Sound absurd? It's not. If you are a Christian, you're illegal too in approximately one-fourth of the world's countries. From Afghanistan to Northern Sudan to China, those who follow Jesus (and in many cases, those who follow any religion except the one approved by their government) are beaten, imprisoned, and even executed for liberties most of us take for granted.

Asia Bibi, a forty-five-year-old mother in Pakistan, had been sentenced to death for her alleged blasphemy against Allah after her conversion to Christianity. How do I know? I served as part of the global outcry for her release, which included activists from a variety of backgrounds, including even Pope Benedict. Her death sentence was revoked due to the international pressure, but the change did not end her plight.

In fact, shortly after this decision, one of the legal leaders in Pakistan who was involved in the case was murdered for his role in the so-called weakening of the nation's strict blasphemy law. In Bangalore and other cities across the nation, demonstrators walked with signs and pumping fists, united to continue the blasphemy laws that put Asia Bibi in jail and on death row in the first place.

What would it be like to live as a Christian in a land where to simply worship Jesus, pray, or read the Bible could cost you your life? Personally, how would you respond if Asia Bibi were *your* mom, sister, or friend?

It's when I began looking at headlines about women like Asia and asked myself, *What would I do if she were my sister?* that I realized something needed to be done and that God wanted me to be the one to do something.

EACH OF US CAN MAKE A DIFFERENCE

There is an initial sense of injustice when we hear of stories concerning Christians mistreated or abused because of their faith, yet this sense of injustice is often quickly replaced with discouragement. We see the problem but do not see how we personally can do anything to change the situation. It seems nothing you or I can do could keep the next church from being bombed in Iraq or Chinese house-church members from being arrested the next time they are discovered.

But that's where we're wrong. In each of the countries where Christians are suffering and in additional nations where persecution takes place on a smaller scale, individuals, families, and organizations are working together to pray, change laws, create safe places of refuge, provide needed aid, and do whatever else is necessary to help those suffering for their beliefs. As a result, many lives are being changed and saved.

How do I know? A friend of mine named Bill[1] leads a children's organization to help kids in poverty in the developing world. In one of those nations, he discovered wide-ranging debt bondage slavery, which affected many of the children in one particular area he had traveled to help. He initially developed a plan to free child slaves, but what he discovered in the process was that the majority of the slaves in this particular area were also those who were Christians. The slave masters felt that holding slaves who shared their own religion was inappropriate but apparently had no problem enslaving children whose families loved Jesus.

Bill is quietly working to free hundreds of these kids and their families. He often works discreetly and behind the scenes, but his work is changing and saving lives among those suffering in the persecuted church.

Another friend, Christopher,[2] has provided aid in the war-torn Sudan region in the name of Christ. While the widespread military violence and associated strife has affected those of all religious backgrounds, Christians are frequently targeted in acts of violence and even forced to serve as child soldiers. Christopher has worked to help those of all backgrounds because of his love for Christ. The efforts by Christopher and many like him have saved the lives of countless individuals, recently resulting in the creation of a new free state, now called Southern Sudan.

Some of those working to aid the persecuted may be closer than you think. First, many American cities host immigrants or international students who cannot openly practice Christianity in their home country. International Students Inc. (ISIOnline.org) offers an entire ministry devoted to serving international students. The Navigators, InterVarsity, Cru (Campus Crusade), and other Christian student organizations on American and Canadian campuses offer similar options.

Second, global technology makes communication possible with those in closed countries. E-mail, videoconferencing, and other technologies allow me to sit at my computer and share the gospel or answer

Bible questions with people anywhere in the world. However, a word of caution. Personally, I have many friends and contacts in nations across Southeast Asia who must practice their faith very quietly to stay out of legal trouble or serious persecution. I'm very careful with what I say in my communications and pray for their safety regularly. Whether you know it or not, your social network of friends likely includes at least a few people in similar situations.

DEFINING PERSECUTION

Before moving further, let me first be clear. When I speak of religious persecution, I am addressing situations in which Christians are discriminated against physically because of their faith. I understand that many would consider the loss of certain American religious liberties such as prayer in school or the removal of a cross from government property as religious persecution, but that's not what is being addressed in this chapter. Americans (and those in the Western world in general) are not typically given bloody noses or broken legs for being baptized or reading the Bible, nor are we put in jail or sentenced to death for declaring that Jesus is Lord. Yet in many countries, this is the case. These are the situations addressed here. American religious liberty concerns tend to be more related to legal issues and, although important, are not the same as the physical suffering endured by believers in Afghanistan or Eritrea.

The International Day of Prayer website (IDOP.org) offers perhaps the most comprehensive biblical list of religious persecutions. Although these could apply to any person in any nation, they are especially in action in nations that legally restrict religious freedom. They include:

- By slander/evil report (see Job 19:18; Psalm 31:13; Luke 6:22)
- Falsely accused (see Psalm 27:12; 35:11; Matthew 5:11; Mark 14:55-60; Luke 23:2,5,10; Acts 6:13; 16:19-23; 26:2,7)

- Ensnared through deceit, trapping, tricks (see Daniel 6:4-5; Matthew 10:16-18; Luke 11:54)
- Designated an object of conspiracy (see Genesis 37:18; 2 Samuel 15:12; Acts 9:23; 2 Corinthians 11:32)
- Mocked, scorned, scoffed, and sneered at (see Job 12:4; Psalm 42:3; Matthew 27:29,31,41; Acts 2:13; 17:18,32; Hebrews 11:36)
- Despised, held in contempt for, loathed, thought nothing of, considered without honor (see 1 Corinthians 1:28; 4:10)[3]

To illustrate the extent to which modern-day religious persecution exists, we can look to Open Doors USA's 2011 Religious Persecution Report:

> The most dangerous countries in which to practice Christianity are overwhelmingly Islamic ones. Of the top 10 countries on the 2011 WWL [World Watch List], eight have Islamic majorities. Persecution has increased in seven of them. They are Iran, which clamps down on a growing house church movement; Afghanistan, where thousands of believers cluster deep underground; and Saudi Arabia, which still refuses to allow any Saudi person to convert to Christianity. Others are lawless Somalia, ruled by bloodthirsty terrorists threatening to kill Christian aid workers who feed Somalia's starving, impoverished people; tiny Maldives, which mistakenly boasts it is 100 percent Islamic; Yemen with its determination to expel all Christian workers; and Iraq, which saw extremists massacre 58 Christians in a Baghdad cathedral on Oct. 31. Of the top 30 countries, only seven have a source other than Islamic extremists as the main persecutors of Christians.
>
> The top 10 in order are North Korea, Iran, Afghanistan, Saudi Arabia, Somalia, Maldives, Yemen, Iraq, Uzbekistan and Laos, which has a Communist government. Iraq is new to the top 10 list while Mauritania dropped out, going from No. 8 to No. 13.[4]

Even the recent revolution in Egypt has been affected by religious persecution involving Christians. In the 2010 U.S. Report on International Religious Freedom, we find that the 2010 bombing, which targeted Coptic Christians, played a pivotal role in leading toward the February 2011 demonstrations and ultimately resulted in the change of national leadership.[5] Religious persecution is a foundational human-rights issue impacting the core of individuals and foreign policy in our world today.

But are Christians *really* suffering and even dying for their faith on a large scale? A quick scan of recent news featured regular persecution and even martyrdom. In Syria, "Christians are under particular assault. Two car bombs detonated in the Damascus suburb of Jaramana November 28 [2012]. Thirty-eight were killed and more than eighty were injured."[6]

The Voice of the Martyrs, an organization that aids Christians around the world being persecuted for Christ, reported that in Kenya, "on Sunday morning, Nov. 4, suspected Muslim extremists hurled a grenade onto the roof of the Utawala Interdenominational Church, killing a police chaplain and injuring at least 11 others."[7]

I'm sure Christopher had no idea when he first stepped off a plane into Sudan's strife that his work would contribute to creating a new nation, but God's plans are often far beyond ours. And Bill did not plan on becoming an abolitionist when his work first led him to help poor children in Asia, but God is using him to save lives among a variety of people, including those who suffer in the name of Jesus. One person can make a difference. I can. You can. And together the difference we make will be much greater than if one of us shrugs our shoulders in defeat before even trying.

HOW YOU CAN HELP

Mother Teresa was known for saying that small deeds done with great love can change the world. In the case of religious liberty, this is certainly true. Occasionally, a new country will result or a law will change, but most efforts will involve smaller-scale work with individuals, families, and churches to help those who suffer for their faith.

A single river separates North Korea from China. Some North Korean parents suffer so greatly that they see "the river" as the only option for their children. Parents will secretly place their children, some as young as three years old, on a small raft and send them to the Chinese side. Their final instructions to their kids are to look for the houses with the small cross. Why? Because the news has spread that persecuted Christians in this region of China will take in refugee children and show them compassion. This is their reputation. This is what they are known for among many North Koreans.

How would you like to be known as one of those people living in the houses with the small cross on them? This is what God has called you and me to be among those suffering for their faith. There are countless ways to help, but many of us do better when given specifics. I want to share some of the ways I've learned—both from others and through my own efforts—to live an Activist Faith lifestyle toward those without religious freedom.

- **Practice devoted prayer.** Prayer is critical for life; devoted prayer is required for religious freedom. God tells us to ask and we will receive (see Matthew 7:8) and that we have not because we ask not (see James 4:2). On a personal level, we can incorporate prayer for the persecuted church and persecuted Christians into our daily prayer time. This is helpful to them and serves as a reminder for us.

  Each year, thousands of churches participate in an International Day of Prayer for the Persecuted Church. At IDOP.org, you can sign up for prayer updates, bulletin inserts, testimonies, opportunities for financial giving, and stories from those in the persecuted church. If your church is not already involved in this movement, be the one to bring it up. Even if your church doesn't decide to participate, you can still have your small group or a group of friends specifically pray for and serve those persecuted because of their beliefs using this or another resource to help.

- **Be a voice.** Many people don't help persecuted Christians simply because they do not know they exist. How will they find out unless we tell them? To be a voice means to use the ways you communicate to share the need to help persecuted believers. If you use social media, talk about how to help persecuted believers in some of your updates and post relevant articles. If you're a blogger, go to OpenDoorsUSA.org and sign up to receive free article ideas to blog about regarding the persecuted church. This is a great way to talk about the issue in depth and help another organization in the process.

  If you're more of a people person, you can talk about the persecuted church among your off-line friends and in your small groups, community groups, school, church, family, office, or wherever else life takes you. The point is to bring up the issue, as many don't know about it. To act, you must first be aware.
- **Show a film.** If you are a film person, you can host a screening of a movie related to the persecuted church. This can be as small as you and a friend at home or as huge as a community-wide event. ChristianCinema.com has an entire list of feature films under the search "persecuted church." Open Doors USA (OpenDoorsUSA.org) also offers a television series that explores the underground church in various countries.
- **Write to prisoners.** At PrisonerAlert.com, you can write a letter to the persecuted believer listed each month. This is an opportunity to encourage believers imprisoned for their faith in a very personal and direct way.

  Just this week, I wrote a quick note to an imprisoned

believer in Afghanistan named Said Musa to encourage him to remain strong. I also blogged a brief article to help others know of his situation and do something. It took all of fifteen minutes.

Some activist groups, such as Amnesty International, have conducted massive letter-writing campaigns for a variety of activist causes that have been extremely effective in the release of prisoners. Do not underestimate the power of your letters. You can change a life today just by picking up a pen or typing a few words on your computer keyboard.

- **Get educated by reading.** Books abound on the issue of religious liberty and persecuted believers, but a few classics stand out. The oldest major book on this issue is *Fox's Book of Martyrs*. It exists in numerous editions, but just about any Christian bookstore has a copy and you can read older versions for free online. It chronicles the early-church tradition about the deaths of the apostles through the time of the Protestant Reformation.

The JESUS FREAKS series of devotional books created with dc Talk and The Voice of the Martyrs offers numerous accounts of modern-day persecuted believers. The books have led many people into missionary service or toward serving the needs of persecuted believers.

As many have documented, in our generation persecution frequently takes place in Muslim-led societies. Emir Caner, a former Muslim-turned-Christian university president, and Edward Pruitt have written *The Costly Call* and *The Costly Call, Book 2* to document some of the stories of persecuted believers from these nations.

Other recommended books include *The Persecuted Church Prayer Devotional*, by Beverly Pegues, and *Safely Home*, by Randy Alcorn, which portrays the story of a believer in the Chinese persecuted church. The real-life story and film *End of the Spear*, by Steve Saint, is an inspiring account of missionaries who gave their lives for the cause of Christ and what God did as a result.

- **Equip your kids.** If you are a parent of young children, KidsofCourage.com offers a tremendous online resource for teaching your children about the issue of persecuted Christians in today's world. It includes materials for use in a family setting, a kids' class at church, a Christian school, and even Vacation Bible School.
- **Send a Bible or aid supplies.** At BiblesUnbound.com, you can donate money to send Bibles to nations where believers are persecuted. Why is this important? In these nations, people cannot buy Bibles themselves; they must be brought in from outside sources. For those already without money for daily needs, this means that many persecuted believers will never have a Bible unless someone like you or me pays to get them one.

  Maybe you have several Bibles in multiple translations at your home, not including access to numerous online versions. Imagine trying to grow as a Christian with *no Bible at all.* Even a small gift can make a big difference. At BiblesUnbound.com, sending one New Testament to a persecuted believer costs an average of only six dollars.
- **Send Christian education resources to persecuted believers.** Love Packages is a ministry focused on putting Christian literature and Bibles into the hands of people around the world. They send these materials to ministries in many poor countries to distribute freely to people hungry for the Word of God. Instead of selling your materials and resources, you can donate new or used Bibles, tracts, reference books, commentaries, Christian books, and more. For a complete list of needed materials and for more information, visit LovePackages.org. Take an opportunity to make a difference

by using what you have to help someone else.

In Luke 3:10-11, we find a great principle taught by John the Baptist that can be applied in this context. The crowd asked John, "What then should we do?" He answered, "Whoever has two coats must share with anyone who has none; and whoever who has food must do likewise." The same could be said of our many Christian books. I dare you to send this book when you're done with it! Who knows how God will use it to encourage someone in another part of the world?

- **Volunteer (here or internationally).** There is nothing like going *to* persecuted believers to help. However, this is not always possible. Many creative options exist. First, you can volunteer at the offices of an organization that supports persecuted believers. One example is The Voice of the Martyrs (Persecution.com), which offers volunteer roles at their U.S. headquarters in Oklahoma. Similar organizations offer many volunteer opportunities or internships, including some that can be done from where you live. You won't know if you don't check!

  Beyond the office, there are also some ways to physically serve among persecuted believers. One example is to serve internationally in business or education in nations where missionary activity is limited. Teaching English in China (see especially ELIC.org) or working for a business in Bahrain for a period of time offers a great opportunity to support those in persecuted situations.
- **Give financially.** Those of us blessed with relative abundance have many opportunities to give financially to support persecuted believers. Whether you give through your own church's denomination or through an organization specifically focused on helping the persecuted church, every penny helps make a difference. Three major organizations in North America that I recommend are Open Doors USA

(OpenDoorsUSA.org), The Voice of the Martyrs (Persecution.com), and International Christian Concern (Persecution.org).

These ten opportunities are more than any one person can handle, but we can all do at least one of them. Combined, our efforts will change the lives of the persecuted church.

Asia Bibi, mentioned at the beginning of this chapter, had her death sentence overturned as a result of people like you and me speaking out on her behalf. Many suffer today, but through the efforts of a multitude of faith activists, lives are being changed and saved.

When I look at Asia Bibi, Said Musa, and other suffering Christians as my brother, sister, or mother, I cannot help but act. They are both my family and my neighbor. As Jesus said regarding the actions of the Good Samaritan, the true neighbor is the one who acts and shows compassion. In His words, "Go and do likewise."

THINK IT THROUGH

Take a few minutes to digest what you've learned and answer the following questions. If you're reading this as a group, talk through your thoughts together.

1. Why do you believe that many Christians aren't more involved in helping persecuted believers? How has this chapter opened your eyes to the struggles Christians face around the world?
2. Many ideas for involvement to help persecuted believers were shared in this chapter. Which of the ideas do you think you could do well?
3. What are some ways you could help your Christian friends become more aware of the need to help persecuted believers? How could you encourage others to become involved in helping those persecuted for their faith?

HELPFUL TOOLS AND RESOURCES

For Research

- *Tortured for Christ*, by Richard Wurmbrand (Hodder Christian Books, 2004)
- *Serve God, Save the Planet*, by J. Matthew Sleeth, MD (Zondervan, 2007)
- JESUS FREAKS, by dc Talk and The Voice of the Martyrs (Bethany, 2005)
- *The Privilege of Persecution*, by Carl Moeller and David W. Hegg (Moody, 2011)

For Action

- Visit bibledude.net/activistfaith to learn more about how you can get involved locally and internationally.

CHAPTER 10

(MODERN) FAMILY MATTERS

MODELING AND MENTORING PARENTHOOD AND SEXUALITY FOR A NEW GENERATION

Daniel Darling

> We live in an age in which we are continually being torn away from that which is priceless and enduring. This means that ours is the task of reminding ourselves, and each other, not only of what we have lost but of what, when it comes to marriage and the family, is still ours to regain.
>
> —William Bennett

When Lyndon Azcuna was only five years old, his father died, leaving a gaping hole in the impressionable boy's life. At the age of seventeen, Lyndon fathered a child out of wedlock, abandoning the child and her mother. Later, Lyndon married and started a family, but he still carried the scars of a fatherless childhood. "I didn't know it, but I brought with me all the pain of losing my dad. I wasn't prepared for leadership in my home." After seven years of marriage, Lyndon walked away. He moved out of his house. But one day, in the midst of a three-month separation from his wife, Lyndon visited his two young girls. Azcuna described this moment: "As I bent down to kiss them goodnight, the Spirit of the Lord whispered to my heart, 'Lyndon, do you really want to see these two girls endure the same pain you suffered without a father?'" This moment was the catalyst for tremendous change in Azcuna's life. Not only did he repent of his broken commitment but he worked to restore his marriage and then began a lifelong commitment to fatherless children. Today, Lyndon Azcuna serves as president of Awana Lifeline, a new ministry whose theme is reuniting children with their fathers, particularly in America's toughest environments, such as the notorious Angola prison in Louisiana (more on this program in chapter 11). I've met Lyndon, and his enthusiasm for fatherless children is infectious. He told me, "Eventually, we hope this ministry will reach many different places where fathering and/or fatherhood is either broken or completely absent."[1]

Lyndon Azcuna is an example of both the tragedy and hope of America's changing family dynamic. It's no secret that the family, as we've always known it, is undergoing a serious makeover. Today more than half of reported births to American women under age thirty occur outside of marriage.[2] In 1960, married families made up almost three-quarters of all households, but by the census of 2000, they accounted for just 53 percent.[3] By the 2010 census, only one in five U.S. households consisted of a married mother and father and at least one child compared to 43 percent of U.S. households in 1950. Forty-one percent of U.S. babies are born out of wedlock. In the African-American community, a staggering 73 percent of children are born out of wedlock.[4]

So what do Christians do? Ever since former Vice President Dan Quayle made family values a centerpiece of his campaign, the family has been at the forefront of America's most vitriolic public debates. In recent years, the debate has reached a fevered pitch with fast-food boycotts, ballot initiatives, and apocalyptic pronouncements. Both political parties have used the idea of family values to drive deep wedges into the American culture. There are few subjects more potently divisive than the ones that touch the family, whether it's the rising fatherlessness crisis, the redefinition of marriage, or the dependency culture that breeds generations of poverty and crime. But the truth is that a very real crisis is emerging in the riptide of this massive social change. And the church, God's called-out people, is well equipped to bring healing and hope to a broken culture.

For younger generations of evangelicals, there exists a certain wariness about culture wars fought over definitions of marriage. Many are openly questioning whether the church should continue to speak up about marriage, sexuality, and family structure. The shrill, inarticulate power grabs of previous Christian leaders have left many with a poor taste in their mouths.

But there are two reasons serious followers of Jesus should care not only about the welfare of their own families but also about the broken homes in local communities and across the nation. The first is theological and the second is sociological.

WHY THE FAMILY MATTERS TO GOD

The concepts of marriage, sex, and parenting all find their root in the opening pages of Scripture. After all, the triune God created the first human, uniquely bearing God's image (see Genesis 1:26). Into man was breathed the "breath of life," and implanted in the human was "a living soul" (2:7, MSG). Humans are considered by God more precious than the rest of His created order. With painstaking detail, God wove the DNA of each human soul (see Psalm 139). If humans are God's image bearers, then His purposes in creating the family unit are intentional, not simply for our own thriving but to reflect His glory.

Andrew Root—associate professor of youth and family ministry at Luther Seminary in St. Paul, Minnesota—wrote this: "God, himself in triune relationship, spoke creation out of nothingness for the sake of relationship. In the same way, in his or her beginning, every child is meant to be welcomed into the beauty of existence through the embrace of mother and father."[5]

Marriage matters and family matters because the intimacy a man enjoys with a woman is God ordained. In Genesis 2:18, we see a profound statement of God's intention: "It is not good that the man should be alone." This is the only time in all of His creation narrative that God declared something "not good." Why? This is not only an indictment against human isolation but also a powerful picture of what God is like. The family unit—man, woman, children—is a reflection of the intimacy of the Trinity. Author and pastor Ray Pritchard wrote this: "There is a part of God's image which is reflected in the coming together of a man and a woman. When man and woman come together, they imitate God in their creative activity. In the bringing forth of new life, they are doing what God did in the Garden of Eden."[6] Man and woman were made distinctly yet complementary to each other (see 1 Corinthians 11:9) and were created to create, like their Creator. This tells us three things.

First, gender confusion that preaches sameness of man and woman is a violation of God's plan. What is humanity? What is mankind? It is man and woman uniting as one flesh. Their union reflects the intimacy shared by the three members of the Trinity. The Scriptures clearly affirm equality of worth and value between men and women, but sameness denies God's creative and purposeful intent for the genders. Second, any sexual intimacy outside of man-woman, one-flesh marital monogamy is deviation from God's design. This is why it states in Genesis 2:24, and is affirmed later by both Jesus (see Matthew 19:5) and Paul (see Ephesians 5:31), "A man shall leave his father and his mother and hold fast to his wife, and they shall become one flesh" (ESV). Last, no other kind of sexual intimacy reflects God's glory. Notice what is written at the end of Genesis 2:20: "For Adam there was not found a helper fit for him" (ESV). No other mate would do. Only a life-long, one-flesh union with a woman reflects God's glory and original purpose for sexuality.

I chatted with Glenn Stanton, director of global formation studies at Focus on the Family, and asked him why he thought marriage was so central to Scripture. He replied,

> In the same breath God creates man and woman, He performs their

> marriage and bids them get started being in the family way. But just as the Scriptures start with a wedding, they also end that way. Look at the last few chapters of the Scriptures, found in Revelation. We find another wedding, but a very different kind. This is where Christ, the long-suffering and faithful Bridegroom, is finally wedded to His beloved, the Church, who has been redeemed from her harlotry and made pure and white.
>
> This is not mere symbolism. It helps us see the very heart and nature of who God is. Marriage, as we experience it, is an earthly picture of a heavenly reality.[7]

For the Christian, the family is a primary way of affirming God's exquisite design and celebrating the beautiful image of His love for the church. I asked renowned speaker, author, and marriage counselor Gary Thomas why he thought marriage was still worth affirming. He told me, "Marriage should be important to Christians because it's important to God. For some reason, God designed most men and women to be married. In affirming marriage, we are bending to God's creative purposes." Thomas also directly linked a marriage message to a gospel message.[8]

WHY THE FAMILY MATTERS TO THE COMMUNITY

But what if this definition of family offends the surrounding culture, a world God has called us to love and serve? I posed this question to Matthew Lee Anderson, a millennial author, scholar, and founder of the blog *Mere Orthodoxy*. He said, "If these ideas are true, if they have such profound impact on society, then we should continue to advocate them. The proclamation of the truth doesn't depend upon the popularity of their ideas or their short-term results."[9]

It's no secret that marriage as an institution is increasingly mocked and belittled in pop culture, academia, and the public square. Yet if God uniquely designed marriage for His glory and as the best instrument for human flourishing, celebrating and advocating a biblical model of the family is one way we love our neighbor. This is how we help shape the culture. This is how we serve the country we love. Denny Burk, associate professor of biblical studies at Boyce College, thoughtfully wrote,

> Our neighbor's good . . . is defined by God, not by our neighbor. That means that from time to time, Christians will love their neighbor by seeking his good even when our neighbor disagrees with what his good is. In the current debate, God defines the good when it comes to marriage. He defines what makes for the health and vitality of the family and the community.[10]

And there is a wealth of data that affirms that the traditional family is crucial for the stability of every community. Children of divorced or never-married mothers have a much higher chance of living in poverty. Half of juvenile criminals grew up in one-parent families.[11] Wayne Grudem, in his book *Politics According to the Bible*, included the work of an anthropologist who, after studying more than eighty failed nation-states, concluded that no society was able to flourish after three generations in which traditional marriage was abandoned as an institution. Grudem wrote, "Every human nation on earth, every society of any size or permanence at all, has recognized and protected the institution of heterosexual marriage."[12]

Perhaps the most tragic fallout of the broken family is the crisis of fatherlessness. Seventy-five percent of high school dropouts, 63 percent of youth who commit suicide, and 75 percent of adolescents at drug and alcohol abuse centers come from fatherless homes.[13] Eighty-five percent of all incarcerated men grew up in a fatherless home.[14]

It's awfully easy to gloss over these statistics because perhaps they don't affect us. But what if each number was the face of a child lacking the nurturing love and care of two committed parents?

THE GOSPEL AND OUR BROKENNESS

So how exactly can people of faith bring healing to a broken family culture? Too often the church has played the role of the Pharisee. In apocalyptic tones, we've used the breakdown of the family as a weapon to bloody our political opponents. Sometimes our affirmation of the high ideal of marriage has come at the expense of the larger narrative of God's redemptive grace in a broken world.

While we shouldn't retreat from cultural conflicts, perhaps it's time to reexamine our tone and articulate our positions in timely, winsome ways. And, like Jesus, we must view the brokenness of our culture as an opportunity to demonstrate God's grace.

After all, Hollywood and Madison Avenue and the ACLU and Democrats are not to blame for the mess America has made of its families. No, the blame goes back thousands of years to a wily serpent and the choice of our first parents, Adam and Eve. Family brokenness in the twenty-first century is not a new phenomenon; it's a tragic by-product of the poison pill of sin, a disease that infects every human heart.

This is why the hope for America's families is not in the next election cycle or ballot initiative or boycott, as important as those may be. The hope is in the coming King, whose reign is both active and yet to come. What our families and culture need most is a supernatural rescue. This Rescuer has come, defeating the sin and death that has pillaged. Jesus is at work making right and putting together what the Enemy has destroyed. And God has commissioned us, Jesus' followers, as healing agents to deliver loving hope for families, the kind of hope that we ourselves have experienced in the midst of our own brokenness.

Specifically, we must address sexual sin with a heavy dose of gospel grace, what J. D. Greear—lead pastor at Summit Church in Raleigh, North Carolina—wrote about in a blog post addressing the issue of homosexuality: "Jesus' central message was not instruction in sexual ethics; it was saving us from ourselves. Study Jesus. And if you conclude, as I have, that He is Lord, then you can and should surrender to Him in all things He teaches, whether you agree with Him or not."[15]

The posture of Jesus' followers has to be twofold. We must lovingly and winsomely uphold the definition of marriage as an ideal worth pursuing so as to contribute to flourishing communities. At the same time, we must also love those who have chosen other lifestyles, we must step into the gap and meet the needs of broken families in our communities, and we must offer a place of hope for those who struggle with sexual temptation of all kinds.

The church cannot simply offer loud indictments of the culture; it must also be a refuge, a way station, where grace fills the gaps. Author Matthew Lee Anderson said, "Christians need to regularly interact with people who are divorced, who are gay, so they can find ways to engage the truth in a way that sounds like good news. The gospel has to be presented as good news. Good news for gay people, good news for straight people, good news for everyone."[16]

The temptation for us is often to remain at arm's length from those who are making unbiblical lifestyle choices. But what our culture needs most is for followers of Christ to embrace those far from God and serve as healers and builders, restoring families one household at a time.

One example of a marriage healer is my friend Bill Yaccino. Bill is a pastor who leads Christ Together, an organization that unites evangelical churches in my community to address community social ills. Several years ago, he launched a website, WeddingPastorsUSA.org. His idea was to be a service to unchurched couples seeking to get married. This not only allows him to help shape the health of future families but it also serves as a gateway for sharing the gospel message. In 2010, Bill spread his marriage efforts countywide. Christ Together offered free marriage enrichment assessments from the Prepare Enrich organization. Churches encouraged Christians to offer this to their friends and neighbors. Two thousand couples took the survey, 54 percent of which were unchurched. Churches also offered a variety of marriage services, from counseling to financial workshops and free date-night babysitting. In 2012, Bill initiated a similar effort, only this time he worked with area businesses to offer discounts for couples' date nights. He said, "What many Christians don't realize is that there are hundreds of couples in their communities who desperately want help with their marriages. The church is in a unique position to help heal those marriages with creativity and compassion."[17]

Bill's work with churches in Lake County, Illinois, is just one of many ways churches around the country can help heal family brokenness. What follows are some other concrete ways to roll up our sleeves and get involved.

HOW YOU CAN HELP

Regardless of cultural trends, God calls every Christian to be a healing influence among the many broken and despairing families in our culture. Imagine how different our communities would look if ordinary Christians rolled up their sleeves and helped rebuild families, one at a time. Here are some ways you might get involved:

- **Faithfully model a Christ-honoring marriage.** Part of the reason many distrust marriage as an institution is that few have seen marriage modeled well. In many ways, Christians have undercut their gospel witness. There is a certain dichotomy about Christians who fight for marriage in the culture but don't fight for it in their own homes. The first place you affect marriage as a cultural institution is in your own home by modeling selfless marriage commitment for your children.
- **Carefully articulate an appealing biblical view of marriage.** Because marriage and family are so valuable to God and society, Christians must still make their voices heard in

our representative democracy and in the culture at large. But in all our engagement, we must do so contrary to the partisan, name-calling, party-hack way we've done it in the past. Gary Thomas said, "I think we do this by reveling in the joy of marriage, by saying to those who don't know the Lord, 'this is what God has done for me.' Sometimes our presentations are so shrill, so caustic."[18]

- **Offer a realistic view of marriage.** One of the most helpful books on this subject is *What Did You Expect?* by Paul Tripp. Unlike most authors, Tripp doesn't present marriage as the pie-in-the-sky source of all bliss. Nor does he offer the usual tips for better communication, sex, and child-rearing. Instead, he goes to the heart of our lofty expectations. Marriage is the union between two sinners who enter into it with significant weaknesses and sin patterns. Tripp argues that a healthy view of marriage sees it not as a vehicle for one's own pleasure and happiness but as an opportunity to demonstrate forgiveness and receive grace. We effectively communicate this idea to others by sharing our own stories of success and failure and by creating safe environments where struggling couples can speak freely and find realistic hope in the gospel.
- **Engage the next generation on the virtues of family and healthy, biblical sexuality.** The church should be proactive in championing purity and the sacred calling of marriage, not only to its own but also to the larger culture. There are several ways believers can do this. First, we must constantly fine-tune our abstinence message. Almost every Christian teen hears from his parents, pastors, and youth leaders the message "Don't have sex." But we must do better explaining why. Teens are bombarded today with a thousand different pressures to treat their purity as something to be bartered. They hear mostly that pleasure is our highest goal. The gospel offers something much more beautiful and liberating: the

opportunity to be free from the enslavement of sexual obsession. Sexuality should not simply be a stand-alone topic in youth group; it should be couched in the context of the larger gospel narrative.

Second, we need to create healthy, grace-based environments. Let's face it: Our kids are not all going to make proper sexual choices because they, like us, are fallen sinners. So while we encourage and teach abstinence, we cannot present it in such a do-or-die way that when they fail there is no place for them to go to find forgiveness and healing. I remember a conversation I had with an older man who was disappointed in the sexual choices his nieces made. I distinctly remember him referring to them as tramps. My heart sank because I wanted to tell him, "Jesus doesn't consider your nieces tramps. He considers them beautiful objects of His love—beautiful yet fallen." As parents, pastors, influencers, and leaders, we should work to create environments where young people can ask questions about sexuality and find forgiveness and grace when they make wrong choices.

Third, we must uphold marriage as a high ideal. Christians are good at talking about abstinence, but we fail when it comes to promoting marriage as a worthy goal. More and more young people are putting off marriage, making their purity pledges more difficult to keep. Many of our youth environments promote irresponsibility and paint maturity and adult relationships as boring and uninteresting. We need to do more than simply keep our kids from having premarital sex; we need to help guide their sexual desire into its God-designed conclusion: marriage. That's not to say we should force or arrange marriages, nor should we make singles feel incomplete, but we should encourage matrimony as a worthy and God-implanted desire.

- **Speak compassionately about the struggle many have with**

same-sex attraction. Many of our Christian brothers and sisters struggle with same-sex attraction. My own father-in-law fought this battle before he died several years ago. I never had the chance to meet him, but my wife shares how deep and painful this struggle was. We should love homosexuals, both those who practice it and those who abstain but struggle with the attraction. We don't have to affirm the sin in order to offer compassionate grace. For many, the struggle is one they didn't choose.

We should also be careful about elevating homosexuality to a level of attention that we don't often give other sins. For instance, we should not treat the gay couple who walks into our churches any differently than we would the unmarried, cohabitating couple. Both need time for the gospel message to take root and the sanctifying work of the Spirit to change their hearts. It's rare for someone who comes to Christ to see immediate victory over entrenched sin patterns, and we should not expect this. Spiritual maturity takes much time and grace.

We should also guard our rhetoric and repent of unkind words. It's important to simply speak the truth and apply it with grace and love (see Ephesians 4:15; Colossians 4:6), keeping our own struggles with sin in mind when we speak about the difficult subject of homosexuality.

- **Become a marriage champion in your community.** This goes beyond the typical marriage ministries most churches have. One ministry doing this is Growthtrac (GrowthTrac .com), which was born out of husband and wife Jim and Sheri Mueller's desire to rebuild families in their own community. They realized that many who look for help begin online, so they built a robust one-stop shop for biblical marriage advice. What began in early 2000 with a six-page website has evolved into a widening ministry that has influenced approximately

500,000 marriages nationwide. Family Life Today and Prepare-Enrich are two other innovative marriage ministries that offer training and help restore marriages in communities around the country.

As you engage in your community, remember that marriage ministry often serves as an evangelistic outreach to seekers. If your church doesn't have a marriage ministry, consider starting one. Or simply begin a small-group study in your local community. You might do something as simple as praying with a husband or wife in crisis or babysitting so they can spend time alone.

In addition to all of this, the church must be a place of grace for those who are experiencing or have experienced the sting of family dysfunction. "One of the things that saddens me," said Sheri Mueller, "is when we find churches shunning couples or families who may be in a deep, dark place, perhaps because the investment would be too difficult or they just don't want to mess with really hurting families."[19] I'm not sure Sheri's experience is the norm around the country, but, regardless, followers of Jesus shouldn't distance themselves from hurting families. We should embrace them and seek to help them find hope and victory in the gospel. For instance, many churches use the Divorce Care ministry to help heal victims of divorce. Other ministries reach out to single parents with assistance and compassionate counsel. These outreaches can be duplicated on a personal, individual level. Your home can be a refuge for a recent divorcee struggling through the implications of her new life. Or you can be a means of spiritual and physical support for a single mom or dad who needs someone to babysit or give rides to children's activities.

- **Be a mentor to a fatherless child.** One of the most pressing needs of our time is for mentors to fill the gaps for fatherless children. This is especially important for young boys, whose lack of a male role model often leads to destructive choices later in life. Fatherless children are everywhere you look, and it doesn't take much to find opportunities for men to step in and serve as surrogate dads. In his book *Father Fiction*, author Donald Miller wrote eloquently about the journey of a boy without a dad. Miller admits that without the presence of influential godly men, he may have ended up where many fatherless boys do: in trouble. So he began The Mentoring Project. His goal is to recruit ten thousand mentors from churches across the country. The idea is to match up a godly man with a needy child and help shape a young man's life. Donald's work has captured the attention of President Barack Obama, himself the product of a dysfunctional family environment. His administration has done great work in helping ministries fill the gap in this fatherless generation. He said,

> We need committed passionate men to serve as mentors . . . even if it's for a couple hours a week shooting hoops, or helping with homework, or just talking about what's going on in that young person's life. Even the smallest moments can end up having an enormous impact, a lasting impact on a child's life.[20]

When it comes down to it, there are two ways Christians can react to the disappointing cultural shifts in the family: We can, like the Pharisees of Jesus' day, curse the brokenness of the culture and take pride in our own better family choices, or we can roll up our sleeves and get involved in healing family dysfunction one home, one couple, one child at a time. Debates over the family will always be present in the public square, but the opportunities for healing and hope will pass if we are content to simply do nothing.

THINK IT THROUGH

Take a few minutes to digest what you've learned and answer the following questions. If you're reading this as a group, talk through your thoughts together.

1. How does the entrance of the gospel story affect your view of family breakdown in our society?
2. In what ways have Christians ungracefully communicated the Bible's definition for marriage and family?
3. How can Christians gracefully address the challenges of the postmodern family structure?
4. What are some practical ways you can be a healing agent for families in your local community?

HELPFUL TOOLS AND RESOURCES

For Research

- On the subject of homosexuality, read J. D. Greear's four-part blog series "Homosexuality, Christianity, and The Gospel" (http://www.jdgreear.com/my_weblog/2012/04/homosexuality-christianity-and-the-gospel-part-1.html) and Joshua Harris's message "Such Were Some of You" (http://www.covlife.org/resources/3965156-Such_Were_Some_of_You).
- For marriage counseling and help, visit GrowthTrac.com and MarriagePartnership.com for a variety of helpful articles and tips.
- For young teens, I highly recommend Dannah Gresh's PURE FREEDOM series (PureFreedom.org).
- Visit bibledude.net/activistfaith for a few more suggestions of excellent resources.

For Action

- For single parents, visit SingleandParenting.org for an entire curriculum and outreach designed with single parents in mind.
- For church or group-based outreach, go to FamilyLife.com for a terrific program that trains couples to be marriage builders. Also, visit Prepare-Enrich.com to be equipped for family ministry.
- Go to bibledude.net/activistfaith to encourage others and advocate for biblical families and sexuality.

CHAPTER 11

BEYOND BIGGER PRISONS

WHERE THE GOSPEL MEETS CRIME PUNISHMENT

Daniel Darling

> The real legacy of my life was my biggest failure — that I was an ex-convict. My greatest humiliation — being sent to prison — was the beginning of God's greatest use of my life; He chose the one thing in which I could not glory for His glory.
>
> — Chuck Colson

Imagine a place where the population has tripled in a little over thirty years and now boasts more than six million.[1] You'd imagine this is a robust, strong, vibrant nation swelling with national pride. But you'd be wrong. The people group I just described, whose numbers continue to soar astronomically, is the expanding prison population (behind bars, on probation, or on parole) in America. According to the book *The New Jim Crow: Mass Incarceration in the Age of Colorblindness*, by Michelle Alexander,

> In two short decades, between 1980 and 2000, the number of people incarcerated in our nation's prisons and jails soared from roughly 300,000 to more than 2 million. By the end of 2007, more than 7 million Americans — or one in every 31 adults — were behind bars, on probation, or on parole.[2]

There's a growing sense among people of faith that we can do better than simply locking up prisoners. What's troubling about the dramatic rise in the prison population is the fact that violent crime has dropped, precipitously, during this same two-decade stretch, meaning that the influx of incarceration involves those who've committed less serious crimes. Political scientist Patrick Egan wrote, "In 2010, violent crime rates hit a low not seen since 1972; murder rates sunk to levels last experienced during the Kennedy Administration."[3]

Some might say that the increased incarceration rates have been the key to fighting violent crime. But in her analysis for *Reason*, Veronique de Rugy wrote, "Research by the Pew Center on the States suggests that expanded incarceration accounts for about 25 percent of the drop in violent crime that began in the mid-1990s—leaving the other 75 percent to be explained by things that have nothing to do with keeping people locked up."[4]

What accounts, then, for the rise in prison population? Most sociologists point to changes in the justice system, begun in the 1980s, that established minimum sentencing guidelines and "three-strikes-you're-out" policies.

What's disturbing about this dramatic increase in incarceration is the seeming profit motive as cash-starved states turn to private companies to run their prisons. In a stunning *New Yorker* exposé, journalist Adam Gopnik wrote,

> A growing number of American prisons are now contracted out as for-profit businesses to for-profit companies. The companies are paid by the state, and their profit depends on spending as little as possible on the prisoners and the prisons. It's hard to imagine any greater disconnect between public good and private profit: the interest of private prisons lies not in the obvious social good of having the minimum necessary number of inmates but in having as many as possible, housed as cheaply as possible.[5]

Sadly, private enterprises profit from a system in which crime increases. Unlike the state, multinational corporations have no incentive to reduce the incidence of crime or rehabilitate criminals. Conservative legal scholar John Whitehead summed it up best: "This perverse notion of how prisons should be run, that they should be full at all times, and full of minor criminals, is evil."[6]

CHRISTIANS AND THE JUSTICE SYSTEM

As I outlined in chapter 2, Christians believe that the government has the right and duty to protect its citizens and enforce its laws. Christians should support the right of the government to crack down on crime and establish safe communities. This is the duty of government, granted by God. But because the state is "God's servant," it must wield its power with caution. Paul wrote in Romans 13:4, "[The government] is God's servant for your good. But if you do wrong, be afraid, for he does not bear the sword in vain. For he is the servant of God, an avenger who carries out God's wrath on the wrongdoer" (ESV).

Here Paul clearly outlined the contours of justice. In a fallen world, God establishes authorities for the welfare and safety of its citizenry. For this reason, the state wields "the sword of God's wrath" on those who threaten this good. But, remember, this is a God of justice. Throughout the Scriptures, God's people are implored to both practice and advocate justice (see Amos 5:24; Micah 6:8).

As with any complicated issue, people of faith will likely have divergent views on the specifics of what justice looks like. A society that allows crime to go unchecked can quickly descend into anarchy and chaos. However, as lovers of justice, we must also work to help reform our broken system and reach out in love to the incarcerated. The late Chuck Colson, founder of Prison Fellowship, championed what he labeled "restorative justice."

Christians believe in the possibility of supernatural heart change through faith in Christ. We don't have to simply curse the darkness of crime and evil; we can be part of the solution in the hearts of prisoners. I had a chance to interview Jim Liske, CEO of Prison Fellowship. I asked him about this exploding prison population. He told me,

> For forty years, our society—including the church—has asked, "How do we get bad people out of our neighborhoods?" While we've been asking that question, our prison population has gone from less than 500,000 to 2.3 million. We must learn to ask another question, one based in practicality and in the gospel: "How do we bring good people home?"[7]

What motivates Liske the most is that "seven hundred thousand people are released from prisons every year and come home to our neighborhoods. Over 90 percent of all inmates will eventually be released." Liske asked, "What kind of neighbors do we want them to be?"[8] Prison Fellowship trains and equips prison chaplains around the country and offers hope with their myriad ministries, such as InnerChange Freedom Initiative, the Angel Tree Network, and Out4Life. They also are an effective and powerful influence in calling for prison reform. Liske is hopeful: "The good news is that through the gospel, the hearts, minds, and souls of these men and women can be transformed."[9]

Other Christian ministries are similarly joining the call to help end the cycle of crime and incarceration. In this chapter, I'd like to share a few of these stories and offer opportunities for people of faith to roll up their sleeves and get involved in the rehabilitation and transformation process God is doing in the lives of prisoners.

HOPE IN DARK PLACES

One story is set in what was once the most violent prison in all of

America: Angola, the largest maximum-security prison in the United States. When Burl Cain became warden in 1995, he immediately instituted serious reforms. Most important, he established six evangelical churches, inviting Christian organizations such as New Orleans Baptist Seminary, Moody Bible Institute, Awana Clubs, and others to participate in evangelizing, mentoring, and restoring the hearts of some of the country's most violent prisoners. Cain's work has been featured on national news programs and become a model for institutions around the country.[10] Today Angola is a model of prisoner rehabilitation and restorative justice.

Another prisoner reformer is Manny Mill, founder of Koinonia House, a national ministry that meets prisoners at the gate after release and connects them to churches and individuals who can help them rehabilitate their lives and become productive citizens. Manny's ministry grew out of his own experience behind bars. After a life of white-collar crime, Manny found himself facing a three-year prison term. Though he became a Christian shortly before his sentence, it was in prison that God put in Manny's heart a desire to see the church help prisoners make the transition to a productive, meaningful, purposeful life. It began with Manny and his wife opening up a home for former prisoners in Wheaton, Illinois.

Koinonia House is now an archetype for similar post-prison ministries around the country. It follows two models. One is a family-based ministry in which a Christian family allows an ex-convict into their home for a short-term period, offering mentoring and transitional assistance with such things as job placement, biblical discipleship, and relationship coaching. There is also a church-based model that equips congregations to adopt former prisoners and support them financially with a circle of accountability, the goal being to see them become independent, self-supporting members of the church and community. Koinonia House also works inside prisons, providing necessary coaching for life outside.

In the previous chapter, I featured the story of Lyndon Azcuna. His ministry was launched in response to requests from inmates who deeply desired a reunion with their children. What emerged is Awana Lifeline, which features two unique ministries. The first, Malachi Dads, helps train incarcerated men to be better fathers through discipleship and mentoring materials. Some of the most hardened lifetime criminals are repenting of their sins, asking forgiveness of their children, and continuing a correspondence with them. The second, Returning Hearts, features an annual reunion between prisoners and their children. This effort is currently active in fifty prisons across the country and is growing rapidly. Awana Lifeline uses its vast network of churches to connect willing followers of Jesus as mentors to the nearly two million children and their incarcerated dads.

In its August 11, 2012, issue, *World* profiled WorkFaith Connection, a nonprofit organization based in Houston. This unique ministry connects local businesses with paroled prisoners, helping them find meaningful employment upon release. Each prisoner goes through an eight-day boot camp that teaches them necessary interviewing skills, identifies key talents, and helps prepare them for the job market. WorkFaith also has relationships with community businesses that trust its recommendations for employment. In five years, 1,560 people have graduated from WorkFaith, 75 percent of whom have found jobs and two-thirds of whom have held down jobs for an entire year.[11]

In my local community (Lake County, Illinois), I've been heartened by the work of Lake County Sheriff Mark Curran. Sheriff Curran is a committed follower of Christ who was moved by a conversation with Chuck Colson and a trip to Angola Prison. When Curran returned to Illinois, he drew attention to the plight of prisoners by spending several days in an actual Lake County jail cell.

The last story features the remarkable journey of my late friend Steve Curington. Steve grew up in a Christian home but after college succumbed to the drug culture of his hometown, Rockford, Illinois. Steve endured a ten-year drug addiction that nearly cost him his life, but one day, after a harrowing car accident, Steve found Christ again. Steve's radical transformation made him a sought-after speaker in his local church. Soon he began a small group just for addicts. This group grew into a large local ministry specifically targeting those struggling with chemical addictions. Within a few years, Reformers Unanimous, a nationwide addictions ministry, was born. As of 2012, the ministry boasted seven hundred chapters nationwide, two residential treatment centers, and institutional programs for the incarcerated. Reformers Unanimous is a Bible-based program that connects the people of God to those in their community struggling with addictions. Their treatment centers treat particularly difficult cases and boast an 80 percent success rate. When Steve Curington passed away in 2010, he left a legacy of many thousands of reborn lives and a program that many individuals and churches are using to free people from the power of addiction.[12]

WHAT YOU CAN DO TO STEM THE GROWING PRISON POPULATION

As I researched the growing prison crisis and spoke with prison ministry leaders, one theme emerged: There is a great need for more Christians to get involved. Lyndon Azcuna admits his difficulty in convincing churches to take prison ministry seriously: "Unfortunately, there is a significant social barrier in helping the families of inmates. Many Christians don't want to be associated with criminals. But Jesus Himself was willing to associate with the lowest elements of society in order to show them His love. And so should we."[13] Koinonia House founder Manny Mill is a bit more candid. Prison ministry is "messy, expensive, and time-consuming."[14] Unfortunately, many of the leaders of these vital outreaches struggle to match the unlimited opportunities with the vast need. For Jim Liske, who was a pastor before assuming the role of Prison Fellowship CEO, it first began with personal conviction:

> I had to take Matthew 25 seriously. Jesus wants me to visit the prisoner—along with the hungry, stranger, naked, thirsty, and sick.

> I also needed to figure out that in reality, I was not just serving the people I went to visit or feed — I was encountering Jesus. He was there. I was truly loving Jesus when I loved "the least of these my brothers," the lost and forgotten people of this world.[15]

Liske said that looking afresh at the gospel message provides the humility necessary to see prisoners as worthy objects of our love. "We all must fall at the base of the same cross. Once we acknowledged that we were in the same boat with those we were called to serve, it was easier to be in solidarity with them and live in community with them. More than that, it became impossible to resist."[16]

So how can concerned people of faith join the growing movement to reduce America's prison population?

HOW YOU CAN HELP

There is a growing need for the body of Christ to minister to those in prison. In this work, we live out the ethos of Jesus' mission (see Matthew 25:36). There are many opportunities to help a prisoner. Here are some ideas:

- **Pray and ask the Lord to help you apply your gifts and talents to this work.** When I asked Lake County Sheriff Mark Curran how people of faith could get involved, he surprised me first by saying, "Dan, they should pray and seek God's leading. Each follower of Christ has a specific skill set that could be applied to prison ministry in some way."[17]
- **Join your local prison or jail ministry as a volunteer chaplain.** If your church doesn't have a program, check the other churches in your area. You might also inquire with the local sheriff's office about the possibility of starting a Bible ministry. Prison Fellowship offers training for prison ministry

and has an extensive network of local contacts. Recent studies have shown that frequent visits actually reduce the chances of offenders repeating their crimes.[18] There's nothing like accountability to keep people from returning to wrong actions.

- **Care for the families of the incarcerated.** Consider that for every person in prison, there is a family left behind without a main source of income. Almost two million children have a mother or father serving time.[19] You can easily help these families through a variety of opportunities. The Angel Tree Network helps connect churches and families on Christmas, and many churches go beyond Christmas to offer support and mentoring through consistent relationships with prisoners or by caring for the basic needs of their families while they are in prison. Awana Lifeline offers individuals a unique opportunity to help mentor fathers in prison and their children. You might also contact your local social service agencies to see what programs are available for prisoner families.

  Jim Liske says that perhaps a good first step is to help make your church a safe place for the relatives of inmates—a place where they can say, "I need help," and you and other church members would immediately stand up and reply, "I'll walk with you."
- **Help transition prisoners to everyday life.** Manny Mill tells me that 82 percent of offenders end up back in prison. Many prisoners come from an urban, poverty-stricken context and possess few skills that will help them obtain and keep a job, become spiritual leaders in their homes, and be a benefit to the community. Often the immediate stresses of the workplace, financial obligations, and family relationships drive them back to a life of crime. Says Manny Mill, "Our prison ministries give prisoners a lot of truth while in prison, but that is not enough to sustain them when they are

suddenly given freedom."[20] Koinonia House offers a fencing model that surrounds a prisoner with a community of faith to help sustain their progress and keep them accountable.

If you are interested in establishing a transitional ministry in either your family or your church, Koinonia House offers significant coaching and resources. Jim Liske of Prison Fellowship cautions that post-prison ministry is best done in teams and with the support of the entire local church "because of the natural networks and support systems that each [church] has. Ideally, the community of Jesus embraces a returning citizen with hope, love, joy, peace, and accountability. Lives change and no one person carries the load alone. The community shares the weight."[21]

- **Employ ex-prisoners.** Ex-prisoners are often caught in a vicious cycle. One of the most stabilizing forces in a new life is a good job, yet they can't find a good job because of their criminal record. If you own a small business, you may be in a position to help change the course of someone's life. It's wise to partner with a credible, recognized organization to vet any ex-offender you might hire, so be sure to contact a local ministry such as WorkFaith Connection. By hiring this way, you may also be able to advance the kingdom as you give back to your community by serving as a mentor to honest ex-prisoners seeking to acquire important skills necessary to thrive in today's workplace environment.
- ❄ **Become a mentor.** In chapter 10, we discussed the power of mentoring. As we documented, the majority of inmates are men from fatherless homes. You might volunteer to mentor a recently released prisoner or you might step in and mentor the children of prisoners who face life without their father in the home. The Mentoring Project or your local Boys & Girls Clubs are excellent sources of information and opportunities

for mentoring. You might also get to know the local parole officers, as they may be able to help you get directly involved in the lives of prisoners.

- **Support reform efforts on the local and national level.** This is an area in which evangelicals have not been as intentional in making their voices heard. If you feel as though you're behind on the facts of the issue, visit the websites of Justice Fellowship and other organizations who champion restorative justice. Christians—lovers of justice—should add this issue as one about which they engage the wider culture.

It seems like tall odds: one person against six million. But what if God is calling you to affect only one life, perhaps a prisoner open to hearing the message of God's love or a child whose father is kept behind bars? God is calling His people to step behind the iron bars and into the lives of needy inmates.

THINK IT THROUGH

Take a few minutes to digest what you've learned and answer the following questions. If you're reading this as a group, talk through your thoughts together.

1. What is the typical cultural attitude toward prisoners?
2. How should the gospel shape the church's response to the prison population?
3. Why is prison ministry often "messy, expensive, and time-consuming"?
4. What can you do to be a healing agent for the prison population in your community? Which groups or organizations could you or your church partner with?

HELPFUL TOOLS AND RESOURCES

For Research

- MartyDuren.com (specifically by searching for "our comfortable injustice"), for information on the exploding prison population
- *The New Yorker* article "The Caging of America," by Adam Gopnik (http://www.newyorker.com/arts/critics/atlarge/2012/01/30/120130crat_atlarge_gopnik#ixzz23YV58qmI)
- *Cain's Redemption: A Story of Hope and Transformation in America's Bloodiest Prison*, by Dennis Shere (Northfield Publishing, 2005), the incredible story of Burl Cain and the Angola Prison

For Action

- Get involved with Awana Lifeline (AwanaLifeline.org). I also encourage you to read the positive review of this ministry in *USA Today*: http://usatoday30.usatoday.com/news/nation/2010-06-17-prison-dads_N.htm.
- Go to PrisonFellowship.org and click on "Get Involved" for a list of helpful resources and links.
- Visit KoinoniaHouse.org for information on how you can volunteer to help prisoners transition to normal life.
- Visit AngelTree.org to find out how your church can minister to prisoners' children at Christmas.
- Start a local Reformers Unanimous (ReformU.com) chapter in your church or order the curriculum to use in your small group or individually.
- Go to bibledude.net/activistfaith to join others in prison ministry outreach.

CHAPTER 12

A THEOLOGY OF ORPHANS

WHY THE CHURCH IS UNIQUELY POSITIONED TO ANSWER THE ORPHAN CRISIS

Dan King

Is it not true that in you the orphan finds mercy?

— Hosea 14:3 (MSG)

The hunger for love is much more difficult to remove than the hunger for bread.

— Mother Teresa

So what does it take to get a man to leave a comfortable job, turn his life upside down, and dedicate the rest of his life to helping little kids in another country? I don't know about you, but it would take a good-sized smack upside the head for me to do something like that. And if I'm right about you, then you're probably pretty much the same.

But that's exactly what happened to Chris Marlow.

He had a meaningful job as a church planter, a job he loved and felt really blessed to have. But he had an experience that rocked his world, and he knew that things could never be the same again.

Today Chris runs an organization called Help One Now. Their mission statement identifies them as "a catalytic tribe committed to caring for orphans and vulnerable children by empowering and resourcing high-capacity local leaders in order to transform communities and break the cycle of extreme poverty."[1]

There's something amazing about Chris's story. As you read my conversation with him, try to put yourself in his shoes. What would you think about the experiences he had? How would they make you feel? How do you think you'd respond?

Dan: So, Chris, I know that this whole thing really started for you during a trip to Africa. Tell me about that experience. What was it like when you arrived?

Chris: We hopped off our plane in Johannesburg, picked up our rental car, and began the long drive into Harare, Zimbabwe. As we drove, I noticed the large sprawl of the city—cars, buildings, freeways. I felt like I was in L.A., not Africa.

We headed to the border and along the way we picked up John and Orpah. Little did I know that in just a few days, John and Orpah would become heroes to me.

At this time, Zimbabwe, once the breadbasket of Africa, was known not for what it had, or used to be, but rather for its extreme poverty. It was a country on the verge of becoming a failed state and a country that had no economy, little food, no gasoline to drive. The political tension could be cut with a knife.

Dan: I know that's the kind of Zimbabwe that we hear about in the media. I'm sure it can be a pretty rough place to be, considering the current state of their economy and the political atmosphere. But you got to experience a different side of the country, right? Tell me about that.

Chris: Yeah, these are the stories that are told on CNN, BBC, and NPR. But those people have never met John and Orpah. While still in South Africa, we filled multiple jerricans with gas, loaded the van with as much rice and beans as possible, picked up a few toys, and headed to the border. In just a few short hours, I would meet thirty orphans whom John and Orpah helped to rescue.

Dan: I love this! I've always believed that some of the best stories of hope and redemption come from the darkest places and situations. People like John and Orpah usually do whatever they can for other people, don't they?

Chris: That's right! After driving frantically for hours under the starry night of Zimbabwe, we finally arrived in Harare, the capital. Our final destination was an hour away. However, Pastor John asked if we could stop to visit some kids who hang out at an abandoned gas station. It was 4 a.m. and we had a van full of food and gas. I was not so sure about all this, but Pastor John insisted, so we did.

Dan: Wow. This would be your first direct exposure to their work, right? What was that like?

Chris: Well, we stopped for maybe three or four minutes. But these would be the three or four minutes that would forever change my life. As I was getting out of the van, we were swarmed with young kids. I felt like a rock star; it was immediate! One nameless young boy grabbed my hand, looked me in the eye with a sense of humility and desperation that I've never seen before, and he said these words that would forever change my life: "Sir, thank you for visiting my country. I'm really sorry it's in the state it's in. I don't want to beg, but I have not had food in days. Is there anything I can do to work for you so I can have a meal?"

Dan: That would break my heart! How did that make you feel, and how did you respond?

Chris: I was confused, overwhelmed, and tired. I looked at this humble boy (created in the image of an almighty God) and said these devastating words: "No, I have nothing for you."

I pulled my hand away from his hand, got back in the van, and drove off into the night. His stare has never left my mind. His voice still echoes in my soul. His pain will always be with me.

As we drove away, I was devastated. No one else in the car knew what was going on. It happened so fast. But for me, it seemed like an eternity, as if an angel showed up in the middle of Zimbabwe to introduce me to something so close to the heart of Jesus: orphans.

Dan: I can totally understand how experiencing a tiny little moment like that can be one of the biggest life-changing experiences in one's life. It sounds like your head (and heart) were going a million miles a minute following that, huh?

Chris: I was having a conversation with God. I was mad, angry, bitter, and broken. How could kids be hungry in such an age of wealth? How did I read Scripture for so long and do so little to care for the orphan? That brief encounter with that unknown, approximately ten-year-old boy is why I started an organization that would "help one now."

Dan: Those are some tough questions to be wrestling with, especially after meeting only one child. But you were on your way to meet several other kids, weren't you? What can you tell me about the rest of that trip?

Chris: As we drove away, it would be just a few more hours until I met thirty more orphaned kids. They had very little in this life. They were crammed in a home, their shoes had holes, their stories seemed straight from the pit of hell: abuse, abandonment, death, rape, suffering, hunger, disease.

I was in Zimbabwe for only a total of thirty-six hours. Since then, I've spent the last several years dedicating my life to serving orphans and solving the global orphan crisis. Instead of thirty orphans, we now have over a hundred kids at that home. They all go to school each day, they smile, laugh, play, and, more important, they know they're loved by many.

Dan: Amen, brother! I know that your efforts are paying off in places like Zimbabwe, South Africa, and a place that I've been a few times: Haiti. But I have to know, did you ever see that one boy again?

Chris: No, I never met that young boy again. I hope someday we will both be walking the streets of heaven. I hope one day I will get to give him a hug, tell him I'm sorry for leaving, and let him know that his story started a movement—a movement that includes caring for orphans all over the world.

Dan: I hope you get that chance too, Chris![2]

It's the butterfly effect! It's the idea that a butterfly in China, flapping its wings, stirs the air, resulting in a chain reaction that eventually causes a hurricane in the Atlantic Ocean.

That one brief experience in Harare, Zimbabwe, would result in children all around the world getting their basic needs met. In fact, not only are they getting fed but there are projects being implemented that will make the situation for the orphans' children less desperate than it is for them.

IF THAT'S NOT REASON ENOUGH . . .

Technically, caring for orphans is not one of the Ten Commandments. However, based on how often the idea is mentioned throughout the Bible, I'd be willing to bet that it would have earned an honorable mention.

Moses shared it among the other laws after sharing the Ten Commandments. Not only did he point out that the orphan should be cared for (along with the widow) but he continued with warnings of a harsh punishment if this law wasn't obeyed (see Exodus 22:21-24).

The command is reinforced several times throughout Deuteronomy, discussed in Job, used as an example in the Psalms, and referenced often by the prophets. Even New Testament writers such as John and James made sure they mentioned proper care for the orphan.

But there is one thing that strikes me more than the mandate in the Word to care for the orphan. It's the realization that *I* am an orphan without God in my life. I know it sounds cliché, but think about this for a moment. Without Christ, we don't have life. We're prisoners to death. There is no redemption, no resurrection, no hope.

However, when we accept Christ into our lives as our Lord and Savior, we are adopted into His family. We have fellowship with our brothers and sisters in Christ and with our (new) Father. We are adopted into His family, and we become heirs of the promise of Life. I love how Paul talked about this concept with the church in Ephesus:

> In love he predestined us to be adopted as his sons through Jesus Christ, in accordance with his pleasure and will—to the praise of his glorious grace, which he has freely given us in the One he loves. In him we have redemption through his blood, the forgiveness of sins, in accordance with the riches of God's grace that he lavished on us. (Ephesians 1:4-8, NIV)

We're adopted! We're no longer orphans! And what's so beautiful about this passage is that we get to see what God's heart is like, which is how we should care for other orphans. How can we lavish grace and love and redemption on the physical orphans of this world?

"UNICEF has estimated that there are approximately 143 to 210 million orphans" in the world today.[3] That's like filling the Rose Bowl stadium to capacity more than two thousand times! But this issue of fatherlessness might be much broader than this number indicates. For now, I'll just say that there's ample opportunity for the church to be working in the area of care for the orphaned and fatherless, and plenty of reasons *why* we should.

THE ISSUE AND THE MOVEMENT

Orphan care is one of the cosmopolitan issues in the church today. It seems that no matter where you go, Christians are tossing around orphan care as one of their most important issues, and that's a good thing. Conferences are popping up all over the place so people can gather to discuss how they'll fix the orphan epidemic.

You don't even have to be in the church to be concerned about orphans. In fact, as high-profile celebrities such as Madonna and Brad and Angelina start adopting children overseas, people take notice. Some may or may not appreciate their (perceived) motive or their method, but their influence is undeniable. Movie and music stars make orphan care cool.

Regardless of the reason this is one of the popular issues of contemporary society, it's still an important one. There are millions of kids who don't know what it's like to have a father, a mother, or both. The family unit is crucial to raising balanced, healthy (physically, emotionally, and spiritually) children. When the family unit breaks down, so do societal foundations, and children who have nowhere to belong are more susceptible to such dangers as human trafficking.

EXPLORING THE OPTIONS

This issue involves more than just sponsoring some poor child overseas through Compassion International or a similar organization. It can even be a little more complex than what many of us are ready for. Let's take a look at some of the situations that fall under this umbrella of orphan care.

International Adoption

Often when we talk about adopting children, we think of bringing children from poor and underdeveloped countries into our American lifestyles. This kind of rescue often results in the child's growing up with a strong family structure, which leads to a greater chance of good health and success. Although international adoption can bring with it many cultural and emotional challenges, there's no denying the difference it can make in a child's life. Studies have shown that "children [who are] placed early in life [do] essentially as well as children raised in untroubled biological homes."[4]

However, there is quite a bit of debate over the issue of international adoption. There's no denying that both the demand for international adoption and the supply of children in developing nations who lack reasonable resources can result in someone trying to profit from it. This can lead to corruption, adoption fraud, and child trafficking.

On one side of the debate, there are people who point to records that indicate that "the abduction, the sale of, or traffic in children" (as outlined by the UN Committee on the Rights of the Child and the Hague Convention) falls within the "most significant category of abusive practices."[5] People on this side of the debate, such as David Smolin from Samford University's Cumberland School of Law, believe that money is the big problem here. In places where most live off a couple dollars per day, the in-country agency receiving somewhere around $20,000 in adoption fees means that adoption can be a very promising business opportunity. This is particularly the case when a child can often be bought (or stolen) for a mere couple hundred dollars from a family who struggles to eat even one meal every few days. Smolin claims that, as a result, "no amount of regulation can overcome the incentives for abuse when such large amounts of money are introduced into vulnerable developing nations."[6] Some on this side of the debate believe that international adoption should be shut down to prevent these kinds of abuses.

On the other side of the debate are those who estimate that instances of children being sold into adoption are much less frequent than what many believe. Further, because of the success rates of children adopted internationally, any incidental fallout of trafficked children still results in a situation that's better for the kids. Elizabeth Bartholet, from Harvard Law School, stated, "Even if adoption law violations occur, the harm such violations cause children and birth parents is minimal compared to the harm caused by shutting down or severely restricting international adoption."[7]

Another alternative that's beginning to emerge in this debate is the focus on in-country adoption. Organizations such as the Kidmia Foundation work to place orphaned children in Ethiopia into the homes of other Ethiopian families. Often they are able to implement community-development programs that allow families to keep their children in their own homes, but in the cases in which adoption is the right solution, they look primarily to in-country adoption rather than sending the kids overseas into another culture. Their goal is to help Ethiopian children become "constructive and productive citizens of their country."[8]

International adoption certainly isn't for everyone. It's likely the most costly way to get involved, and it's a very complex process. Like anything else, the decision to adopt should be centered in prayer, taking into account wise counsel from people who know what they're doing. (See the list of organizations we suggest at the end of this chapter.) One should also consider keeping the family unit intact whenever possible. Keeping a child with his or her birth parents should always be the first choice.

However, when it's right, adoption can be a great option to pursue. Some of the most beautiful families I know are full of different-colored children who act no different than birth-related kids.

Overseas Child Sponsorship

A great way to get involved in the international orphan-care scene is to consider child sponsorship. It allows the child to remain in his or her own culture and often helps maintain the family structure. The models for how it works can be as diverse as the communities they support.

In some cases, child-sponsorship programs help to support actual orphans who live in orphanages. For about thirty to forty dollars per month, you can help provide for basic needs such as food, clothing, and education.

In other cases, organizations work in communities where the children still live with their birth parents. Rather than the money going to the child or their family, it might go to a church or community leader who works to provide for the same basic needs. This is the kind of sponsorship that my family is currently a part of in Haiti. The cumulative sponsorship funds help to provide all the kids a lunch each day while they're in school. Because the community is so poor, this is often the only meal most of these kids receive in a day. Getting more children sponsored in that community means the local leader can begin to look beyond the basic needs and start working on other community-development projects that create jobs and resources that will eventually help break the cycle of poverty.

Either way, this form of involvement is easy and can be very rewarding. Most child-sponsorship organizations will arrange for you to be able to send letters back and forth with the child you're sponsoring. Deep and meaningful relationships can be built fairly quickly through this kind of pen-pal interaction, and it helps you see where your investment in the lives of children is paying off.

Domestic Foster Care

In the United States, the foster-care system replaces the orphanage. Rather than sending children into a central home, they are placed with registered families. Often the children being placed in foster homes have been removed from their homes by Child Protective Services due to their parents being addicted to drugs or incarcerated. With many of these children coming from abusive situations (they were either witnesses to abuse or directly abused) or having been neglected (uncared for and malnourished), they often come into the foster homes with a sense of worthlessness and inadequate social skills.

What's worse is that many of these children can end up in homes that aren't much better. Some studies show that children in foster care suffer from post-traumatic stress disorder (PTSD) just as soldiers returning from war do. That's where the church can fill a big gap. One thing that can bring much-needed structure and healing to a child coming out of a neglectful and abusive environment is a loving home with a strong family structure.

This isn't an option that should be considered lightly. It's not for everyone, but we can support those who are prepared to bring foster children into their homes. Church families are often extended families who can continue to show love toward the children and help them discover a sense of self-worth and belonging that may have been previously missing in their lives. Many churches have special programs and support ministries designed to help foster and adoptive families. It's a great way for us to help carry each other's burdens.

The Christian family may be able to provide a good, safe environment for the child, but the first choice should always be to restore the relationship with the birth parents whenever possible. The reality is that some birth parents will never become fit parents, but those who do clean up their act should have their child returned to them. It can be difficult to let children go when you've poured so much love into their lives, so we need to cherish the time we have with these foster children and pray that the seeds we planted produce good fruit in their lives.

Domestic Adoption

While foster care can often be a temporary experience, there are times when it can lead to full, legal adoption. Sometimes the children are released by the state or parents to officially and permanently become part of a new family. This route is often not as expensive as international adoption, and in many states, the adoption costs are covered by the state when pursuing foster-to-adopt as a solution. The best thing about this approach is that you can provide children with a much greater sense of stability and belonging when you make them a permanent part of your family.

A NOTE ABOUT FATHERLESSNESS

Unfortunately, one doesn't have to live in an orphanage or foster home to suffer from fatherlessness. Sometimes children living in "normal" homes have parents who are physically or emotionally absent.

Being emotionally abandoned can be devastating. Dr. John Sowers reported in his book *Fatherless Generation* that fatherlessness is the driving engine for some of the United States' worst problems: gang violence, high school dropouts, teenage pregnancy, and suicide.[9]

Dr. Sowers' studies show that approximately 71 percent of teenage girls who become pregnant come from fatherless situations. And when you consider that at least a third of teenage pregnancies will end in abortion, the result is somewhere around 250,000 babies aborted nationally each year.[10] We're essentially seeing an abortion problem driven (at least partially) by a root cause of fatherlessness. It seems that if we want to reduce abortions (especially teenage abortions), we have to deal with this issue of fatherlessness.

That's what makes programs designed to give kids a place to go so important. Can you imagine what it would look like if churches started flooding organizations like Big Brothers Big Sisters? The collective positive influence on the future of our local communities could be amazing!

HOW YOU CAN HELP

One thing to consider when working in the area of orphan care is that any approach that doesn't deal with the root cause is incomplete. Sponsoring children as a means of simply getting them something to eat isn't enough. If it's not breaking the cycle of poverty, then it's just a meal on us, so we must make sure that we invest our time and resources into activities and organizations that think and work holistically.

There are far too many organizations doing good work to list here, but if you're looking for a place to start, check out some of these ideas and resources:

- **Pursue adoption.** Organizations such as Show Hope (ShowHope.org) can get you started with the adoption process and help you find the support you need. You can also become an adoption advocate and provide support for those going through the process.
- **Support in-country adoption in other countries.** Kidmia Foundation (Kidmia.org) is doing this in Ethiopia with great results.
- **Sponsor a child.** By working with organizations such as Help One Now (HelpOneNow.org), Compassion International (Compassion.com), and World Vision (WorldVision.org), you can help provide for the basic needs of orphaned and other vulnerable children.
- **Support adoptive parents and ministries in your area.** Look up local adoption agencies and find out what their needs are. You might also be able to help adoptive parents by providing free babysitting and family bonding activities.
- **Be a youth mentor.** Check out Big Brothers Big Sisters (BBBS .org) and The Mentoring Project (TheMentoringProject.org) to become a mentor to a youth in your area, or launch a program at your church that provides a much-needed positive influence in a child's life.

With lots of prayer and love to give, the church can make a major impact on future generations by getting more involved in the area of orphan care.

I sat in the back of a church sanctuary at the end of an emotionally exhausting conference on orphan care when Mike Rusch, the host of the event, brought the attendees' children up on stage to hold up pictures they had just drawn of their families. As we all oohed and aahed over these cute artistic interpretations of family, Mike reminded us that at that moment, there were somewhere around 146 million children who couldn't draw that same picture. Let's make that number smaller.

THINK IT THROUGH

Take a few minutes to digest what you've learned and answer the following questions. If you're reading this as a group, talk through your thoughts together.

1. Consider God's heart for all of us to care for the orphan, yet recognize that we all have varying roles in that call. Prayerfully consider what your role might be. What can you do today to start caring more for orphans?
2. Do you know anyone who has adopted? What are their biggest needs right now? How can you fill them?
3. What organizations in your area work in the field of adoption and orphan care? How can you or your church be a support to foster and adoptive families?
4. Do you sponsor a child? Write a letter to that child today. How can you be more than a financial blessing to that child?

HELPFUL TOOLS AND RESOURCES

For Research

- *Fatherless Generation: Redeeming the Story*, by John Sowers (Zondervan, 2010)

- "The Debate," by Elizabeth Bartholet and David Smolin (http://www.law.harvard.edu/faculty/bartholet/The_Debate_1_13_2012.pdf)
- *Orphanology: Awakening to Gospel-Centered Adoption and Orphan Care*, by Tony Merida and Rick Morton (New Hope Publishers, 2011)
- *Reclaiming Adoption: Missional Living Through the Rediscovery of Abba Father*, edited by Dan Cruver (Cruciform Press, 2010)

For Action:

- Check out Bethany Christian Services (Bethany.org) and Focus on the Family's I Care About Orphans (ICareAboutOrphans.org) for more ways to make an impact.
- Go to bibledude.net/activistfaith to join with fellow activists in caring for orphans.

FINAL THOUGHTS

When Activist Faith began as a blog on Beliefnet.com, the dream was to launch a place to integrate faith and action on the issues that matter most. More than seven hundred posts and three years later, we've blogged about the Arab Spring, Occupy Wall Street, tornadoes in the U.S., Japan's tsunami, Pakistan's floods, ending modern slavery, providing clean water, feeding the poor, clothing those in need, serving the homeless, and much, much more.

What we've enjoyed most during this time have been the stories of God at work in the lives of ordinary, everyday people to make an impact on others in transforming ways. God repeatedly uses the least-likely and least-prepared individuals (ourselves included) to make the deepest impact on our world. To wrap up our time together, I (Dillon) want to share a few of the lessons we've learned along the journey.

1. People frequently comment on what matters most to them personally. From views on natural disasters to frustrations about abortion to poverty to religious freedom, every person has an area that drives emotions to a level that leads to a response. Our goals for the days ahead? To be more personal in sharing some of what matters to help foster even more meaningful community. You can join the conversations and movement and encourage fellow activists at ActivistFaith.org.

2. Many Christians are often the real leaders in making lasting impact. Yes, church-attendance statistics show decline, and the media frequently choose the loudest voices to represent the faith, yet there are many Christians serving those in need with limited resources, time, and support. Japan's tsunami victims will live differently because of many Christians who helped. The same can be said of Joplin's tornado victims, storm victims in the Southeast, flood victims in Pakistan, those facing famine in the Horn of Africa, those affected by the 2010 earthquake in Haiti, those standing against Christian persecution in the Middle East and North Korea, and the many children around the world sponsored each month by Christians in the U.S. and elsewhere we have been blessed to connect with in our efforts.

3. Much more work remains to be done. Evangelical Christians seem to be just getting started in many issues of social justice. As Christians rediscover the teachings of Jesus related to helping "the least of these" (Matthew 25:40), more and more are getting involved. Whether building friendships with Muslims or building homes in Honduras, whether adopting or sponsoring a child, Christians are becoming more "activist" every day. For the small role I get to play in the process, all I can say is, "Thank You, God."

Also, a big thank-you to every person who has read, shared, posted, contributed, and lived out the posts Daniel, Dan, and I have shared. As the apostle Paul wrote, "I thank my God every time I remember you" (Philippians 1:3, NIV).

After Jesus had cast the evil spirits out of a man in the region of Gerasenes (see Mark 5:1-20), the guy wanted to serve as one of Christ's followers. He had been transformed. He was ready to go anywhere and do anything for the One who had changed him. You would think Jesus would have taken him up on the offer. Instead, he told the man something along the lines of, "Go home to your own people and tell them how much the Lord has done for you and how he has had mercy on you." Instead of complaining, the man obeyed. He spread the news about Jesus among his friends and neighbors.

I talk to lots of people who are ready to become missionaries to the ends of the earth, those ready to move across the country for college or seminary, and others willing to move to the inner city from their small town to become urban missionaries. These are all admirable pursuits, but Jesus might just say no.

As you pray for guidance, consider that Jesus might answer, "I've changed you so you can live out your faith where you currently live, work, and study. Begin right now." Okay, so Jesus did not exactly say it like this in the Gospels, but it's an accurate and realistic paraphrase. You might not like your job, your major, or your place in life at the moment. God might have some big plans for you in another part of the world someday. Until then, start where you are. That's where He's placed you for the moment. Live with Activist Faith.

NOTES

The Other Side of Justice

1. Kristen Scharold, "Tim Keller: What We Owe the Poor," *Christianity Today*, December 6, 2010, http://www.christianitytoday.com/ct/2010/december/10.69.html?start=2#related.
2. "Religion, Politics, and Other Unmentionables: Author Peter Wehner talks with NRO," *National Review Online*, October 11, 2010, http://www.nationalreview.com/articles/248855/religion-politics-and-other-unmentionables-interview.

Chapter 1: Free the Slaves (Again!)

1. Manav Tanneeru, "The Challenges of Counting a 'Hidden Population,'" *The CNN Freedom Project: Ending Modern-Day Slavery* (blog), CNN, March 9, 2011, http://thecnnfreedomproject.blogs.cnn.com/2011/03/09/slavery-numbers.
2. "Slavery Today," Free the Slaves, accessed December 13, 2012, http://www.freetheslaves.net/SSLPage.aspx?pid=301.
3. "Fact Sheet: Human Trafficking (English)," Office of Refugee Resettlement, Administration for Children & Families, August 2, 2012, http://www.acf.hhs.gov/programs/orr/resource/fact-sheet-human-trafficking.
4. Beth Burger, "Tennessee Police, Non-Profits to Receive Training on Sex Trafficking from TBI," *Chattanooga Times Free Press*, October 19, 2011, http://www.timesfreepress.com/news/2011/oct/19/tennessee-police-non-profits-receive-training-sex-.
5. Linda A. Smith, Samantha Healy Vardaman, and Melissa A. Snow, "The National Report on Domestic Minor Sex Trafficking: America's Prostituted Children," Shared Hope International, May 2009, http://sharedhope.org/wp-content/uploads/2012/09/SHI_National_Report_on_DMST_2009.pdf.

6. Charles J. Powell, "America's Ugliest Crime," *Charisma*, October 31, 2009, http://www.charismamag.com/life/social-justice/15193-america-s-ugliest-crime.
7. "Trafficking in Persons Report 2011," U.S. Department of State, accessed December 12, 2012, http://www.state.gov/j/tip/rls/tiprpt/2011.
8. Charles Powell, personal correspondence with the author, May 25, 2011.
9. Powell, personal correspondence.
10. Some of these ideas are adapted from my book *Not in My Town* with Charles Powell (Birmingham, AL: New Hope Publishers, 2011).
11. "Slavery Today."

Chapter 2: Immigration Nation

1. "David Morales Wants to Start Utah's Biggest Church," We Are America: Stories of Today's Immigrants, accessed August 6, 2012, http://weareamericastories.org/written/david-morales-wants-to-start-utahs-biggest-church.
2. "Tell ICE to Stop Deportation of 19-Year-Old Aspiring Pastor, David Morales," Change.org, accessed August 6, 2012, http://www.change.org/petitions/tell-ice-to-stop-deportation-of-19-year-old-aspiring-pastor-david-morales.
3. David Montero, "Undocumented Immigration Activist Won't Be Deported," *The Salt Lake Tribune*, February 24, 2012, http://www.sltrib.com/sltrib/politics/53577979-90/activist-agents-case-closed.html.csp.
4. "Few Say Religion Shapes Immigration, Environment Views," Pew Research Center for the People & the Press, September 17, 2010, http://www.people-press.org/2010/09/17/few-say-religion-shapes-immigration-environment-views.
5. Dr. Bryant Wright, "Immigration: A Biblical View," sermon preached on September 4, 2011, http://rightfromtheheart.org/watch/48528.
6. Matthew Soerens and Daniel Darling, "The Gospel and Immigration," The Gospel Coalition, May 1, 2012, http://thegospelcoalition.org/blogs/tgc/2012/05/01/the-gospel-and-immigration.
7. Soerens and Darling.
8. Sarah Pulliam Bailey, "Exclusive: Focus on the Family's Jim Daly on a New Stance on Immigration Reform," *Christianity Today*, June 12, 2012, http://www.christianitytoday.com/ct/2012/juneweb-only/exclusive-jim-daly-on-immigration.html.
9. Matthew Robbins, "Russell Moore on Immigration," June 17, 2011, *Chosen for Grace* (blog), http://www.chosenforgrace.com/2011/06/russell-moore-on-immigration.html?m=1.

10. J. Lance Conklin, in discussion with the author, August 8, 2012.
11. Cathy Lynn Grossman, "Rick Warren Speaks Up on Compassion, Politics, 'Big' Churches," Faith & Reason, *USA Today*, September 20, 2009, http://content.usatoday.com/communities/Religion/post/2009/09/rick-warren-lords-prayer-compassion-illegal-immigration/1#.UCAIujGe5M5.
12. Conklin.
13. Laura Wides-Munoz and Garance Burke, "Undocumented Immigrants Prove Big Business for Prison Companies," *The Huffington Post*, August 2, 2012, http://www.huffingtonpost.com/2012/08/02/immigrants-prove-big-business-for-prison-companies_n_1732252.html.
14. Conklin.
15. Conklin.
16. Matthew Soerens, in discussion with the author, September 2012.
17. Emily McFarlan, "Getting to Know Thy Neighbor," *Courier News*, August 4, 2011, http://couriernews.suntimes.com/4710096-417/getting-to-know-thy-neighbor.html.

Chapter 3: The Poverty Epidemic

1. *Merriam-Webster Online*, s.v. "hunger," accessed December 18, 2012, http://www.merriam-webster.com/dictionary/hunger.
2. "2012 World Hunger and Poverty Facts and Statistics," World Hunger Education Service, updated December 4, 2011, http://www.worldhunger.org/articles/Learn/world%20hunger%20facts%202002.htm.
3. "2012 World Hunger."
4. "Microcredit in Bangladesh 'Helped 10 Million,'" *BBC News*, January 27, 2011, http://www.bbc.co.uk/news/business-12292108.
5. Kelli Ross, "Children of Microfinance: Fernando in Bolivia," BibleDude.net, accessed December 17, 2012, http://bibledude.net/children-of-microfinance-fernando-in-bolivia.

Chapter 4: Created to Care

1. Alexei Laushkin, "Y.E.C.A. Encourages Pastor Rick Warren on Climate Action," Young Evangelicals for Climate Action, July 28, 2012, http://www.yecaction.org/2012/07/28/encouraging-rick-warren-on-climate-action.
2. "Why Creation Care Matters," Evangelical Environmental Network, accessed March 5, 2013, http://www.creationcare.org/blank.php?id=41.
3. Margot Starbuck, "Green Revolution," *Relevant*, March 2, 2011, http://rejectapathy.com/creation-care/features/21689-green-revolution.

4. "Mercury and the Unborn: The End Mercury Poisoning Pledge," Evangelical Environmental Network, May 18, 2011, http://creationcare.org/blog.php?blog=30.
5. "How Much Garbage Does a Person Create in One Year?" WiseGeek, accessed December 12, 2012, http://www.wisegeek.com/how-much-garbage-does-a-person-create-in-one-year.htm.
6. "Conservation Tips," Environment@rtp, accessed December 12, 2012, http://environmentrtp.org/sustainability/conservation-tips.
7. "Water Facts," Detroit Water and Sewerage Department, revised January 2009, http://www.dwsd.org/downloads_n/customer_service/customer_information/waterfacts_09.pdf.
8. "Conservation Tips."
9. Brad Tuttle, "184 Money Tips," *Time*, March 18, 2011, http://business.time.com/2011/03/18/184-money-tips-how-to-repurpose-leftovers-save-50k-and-put-your-preschooler-to-work/#ixzz2ENn9yaLQ.
10. "The Green Office Project: Recycling Matters," Office Supply Services, accessed December 12, 2012, http://www.ossone.com/greenproject.html.
11. "Conservation Tips."
12. "The Green Office Project: Purchase Guide," Office Supply Services, accessed December 12, 2012, http://www.ossone.com/greenproject.html.
13. "Why We Care: Vision and Values," Young Evangelicals for Climate Action, accessed December 12, 2012, http://www.yecaction.org/why-we-care.
14. Morris, "Ed Begley, Jr. in Praise of Energy Audits," Efficiency First, January 5, 2010, https://www.efficiencyfirst.org/blog/2010/01/05/ed-begley-jr-in-praise-of-energy-audits.

Chapter 5: Emergency Response

1. Dino Rizzo, *Servolution: Starting a Church Revolution Through Serving* (Grand Rapids, MI: Zondervan, 2009), 57.
2. Romanita Hairston, in an interview with the author, "Finding Hope in the Tornado Zone [An Interview with @WorldVisionUSA]," video location 9:56–10:21, accessed December 17, 2012, http://bibledude.net/finding-hope-in-the-tornado-zone-an-interview-with-worldvisionusa.
3. Sandro Galea, Arijit Nandi, and David Vlahov, "The Epidemiology of Post-Traumatic Stress Disorder After Disasters," *Oxford Journals*, December 17, 2004, http://epirev.oxfordjournals.org/content/27/1/78.full.

4. Galea, Nandi, and Vlahov.
5. Tom Templeton and Tom Lumley, "9/11 in Numbers," *The Guardian/The Observer*, August 17, 2002, http://www.guardian.co.uk/world/2002/aug/18/usa.terrorism.

Chapter 6: Home Sweet Homeless

1. Noel Brewer Yeatts, *Awake* (Grand Rapids, MI: Baker, 2012), 16.
2. Reuben Cenea, "Joy Through Handicap," Mission of Hope, March 8, 2012, http://www.mohhaiti.org/blog/category/moh_500.
3. Charlie Hughes, "Charlie's Corner," *The Open Door: Newsletter of the Chattanooga Community Kitchen*, Spring 2012, 3, http://www.homelesschattanooga.org/images/Newsletters/Spring2012Newsletter.pdf.
4. Alex Veiga, "Foreclosure Sales Slow, but Remain Very High," MSNBC, May 26, 2011, http://www.msnbc.msn.com/id/43175612/ns/business-personal_finance/#.UECd-0TbDM8.
5. "Overnight Shelter: The Big Picture," *The Open Door: Newsletter of the Chattanooga Community Kitchen*, Winter 2012, 5, http://www.homelesschattanooga.org/images/Newsletters/Winter2012Newsletter.pdf.
6. Mark Horvath, "My First Night Homeless: A True Story," *The Huffington Post*, April 20, 2011, http://www.huffingtonpost.com/mark-horvath/my-first-night-homeless_b_850145.html.
7. Allison J. Althoff, "Food Fights: Homeless Ministries Respond to Restrictions," *Christianity Today*, September 5, 2012, http://www.christianitytoday.com/ct/2012/september/homeless-ministry-restrictions.html.
8. Jeff Tietz, "The Sharp, Sudden Decline of America's Middle Class," *Rolling Stone*, June 25, 2012, http://www.rollingstone.com/culture/news/the-sharp-sudden-decline-of-americas-middle-class-20120622.
9. Stan Friedman, "Church Parking Lot Provides Unique Housing for Homeless," The Evangelical Covenant Church, July 2, 2012, http://www.covchurch.org/news/2012/07/02/church-parking-lot-provides-unique-housing-for-homeless.
10. Gary Warth, "Vista: Safe Parking Lot for Homeless Cited by City," *North County Times*, July 28, 2012, http://m.nctimes.com/news/local/vista/vista-safe-parking-lot-for-homeless-cited-by-city/article_0a17eeeb-0dee-5d9d-b631-3647e1a38394.html.
11. "About Us," Family Promise of Greater Chattanooga, accessed December 16, 2012, http://familypromisechattanooga.com/core-values/about-us.

Chapter 7: The Least of These

1. Michelle Pirraglia, "A Survivor's Story: Choosing Life in a Culture of Death," Patheos, January 24, 2011, http://www.patheos.com/Resources/Additional-Resources/Survivors-Story-Choosing-Life-in-a-Culture-of-Death-Michelle-Pirraglia-01-24-2011.
2. James Hoffmeier, in Randy Alcorn, "When Does Life Begin According To Your Study of Scripture?" January 29, 2010, http://www.epm.org/resources/2010/Jan/29/when-does-life-begin-according-your-study-scriptur.
3. "ANF03. Latin Christianity: Its Founder, Tertullian," Christian Classics Ethereal Library, accessed December 16, 2012, http://www.ccel.org/ccel/schaff/anf03.iv.iii.ix.html?highlight=to,hinder,a,birth,is,merely,speedier,man%20killing#highlight.
4. "NPNF2-06. Jerome: The Principal Works of St. Jerome," Christian Classics Ethereal Library, accessed December 16, 2012, http://www.ccel.org/ccel/schaff/npnf206.v.XXII.html.
5. Randy Alcorn, "Biblical Perspectives on Unborn Children," Eternal Perspective Ministries, accessed December 16, 2012, http://www.epm.org/static/uploads/downloads/biblical-perspectives-on-unborn-children-handout.pdf.
6. John Calvin, *Commentaries on the Last Four Books of Moses*, trans. Charles William Bingham (Grand Rapids, MI: Eerdmans, 1950), 3:41-42.
7. "Fetal Development from Conception to Birth," National Right to Life, accessed December 12, 2012, http://www.nrlc.org/abortion/facts/fetaldevelopment.html. (For a more in-depth study, consider "Human Development: Conception to Birth," Society for the Protection of Unborn Children, http://www.spuc.org.uk/abortion/prenataldevelopment.)
8. Randy Alcorn, "When Does Each Human Life Begin? The Answer of Science," Eternal Perspective Ministries, January 29, 2010, http://www.epm.org/resources/2010/Jan/29/when-does-each-human-life-begin-answer-science.
9. "From the War of Independence to Operation Enduring Freedom—Blood Spilled from Sea to Shining Sea," Military Factory, accessed December 17, 2012, http://www.militaryfactory.com/american_war_deaths.asp.
10. "Facts on Induced Abortion in the United States," Guttmacher Institute, August 2011, http://www.guttmacher.org/pubs/fb_induced_abortion.html.
11. William Cowper, "There Is a Fountain," http://www.cyberhymnal.org/htm/t/f/tfountfb.htm.

12. Jared C. Wilson, "A Gospel-Shaped Pro-Life Passion," *The Gospel-Driven Church*, January 20, 2012, http://thegospelcoalition.org/blogs/gospeldrivenchurch/2012/01/20/a-gospel-shaped-pro-life-passion.
13. Lydia Saad, "'Pro-Choice' Americans at Record-Low 41%," Gallup, May 23, 2012, http://www.gallup.com/poll/154838/pro-choice-americans-record-low.aspx.
14. Lydia Saad, "More Americans 'Pro-Life' Than 'Pro-Choice' for First Time," Gallup, May 15, 2009, http://www.gallup.com/poll/118399/more-americans-pro-life-than-pro-choice-first-time.aspx.
15. "History," Students for Life of America, accessed March 5, 2013, http://www.studentsforlife.org/about/history.
16. Steven Ertelt, "Pro-Abortion Poll Shows Majority of Women are Pro-Life," *LifeNews.com*, June 25, 2003, http://www.lifenews.com/2003/06/25/nat-13.
17. "Creating Effective Messages," Heroic Media, accessed December 12, 2012, http://www.heroicmedia.org/power-of-media/research-and-results.
18. Matt Lewis, "Rick Santorum's Comments on Obama and Abortion—Clarified," *Politics Daily*, January 21, 2011, http://www.politicsdaily.com/2011/01/21/rick-santorums-comments-on-obama-and-abortion-explained/print.
19. "A Passion to Serve: How Pregnancy Resource Centers Empower Women, Help Families, and Strengthen Communities," 2nd ed., Family Research Council, accessed December 17, 2012, http://downloads.frc.org/EF/EF12A47.pdf.
20. Tricia Goyer, *Blue Like Play Dough* (Colorado Springs, CO: Multnomah, 2009).
21. Michael J. New, PhD, "Analyzing the Effect of State Legislation on the Incidence of Abortion Among Minors," The Heritage Foundation, February 5, 2007, http://www.heritage.org/research/reports/2007/02/analyzing-the-effect-of-state-legislation-on-the-incidence-of-abortion-among-minors.

Chapter 8: War, Terror, and Genocide

1. Jonathan Hunt, "Son of Hamas Leader Turns Back on Islam and Embraces Christianity," FOX News, August 12, 2008, http://www.foxnews.com/story/0,2933,402483,00.html and "Mosab Hassan Yousef," Wikipedia, accessed December 17, 2012, http://en.wikipedia.org/wiki/Mosab_Hassan_Yousef.
2. "Just War Theory," Wikipedia, accessed December 17, 2012, http://en.wikipedia.org/wiki/Just_war_theory.

3. "Genocide," Wikipedia, accessed December 17, 2012, http://en.wikipedia.org/wiki/Genocide.
4. "Genocides in History," Wikipedia, accessed December 17, 2012, http://en.wikipedia.org/wiki/Genocides_in_history.
5. "Spirituality and Trauma: Professionals Working Together," National Center for PTSD, United States Department of Veterans Affairs, accessed December 17, 2012, http://www.ptsd.va.gov/professional/pages/fs-spirituality.asp.

Chapter 9: Why I Am Illegal in More Than Fifty Countries

1. Name has been changed to protect his work in the countries in which he operates.
2. Name has been changed to protect his work in the countries in which he operates.
3. "Bible Readings: Some Possible Forms That Persecution May Take," International Day of Prayer for the Persecuted Church, accessed December 16, 2012, http://idop.org/pages/resources/bible-readings.php.
4. Dillon Burroughs, "2011 Religious Persecution Report," Beliefnet, January 2011, http://blog.beliefnet.com/activistfaith/2011/01/2011-religious-persecution-report.html#ixzz1EDt5mTOu.
5. "International Religious Freedom Report 2010: Egypt," U.S. Department of State, November 17, 2010, http://www.state.gov/g/drl/rls/irf/2010/148659.htm.
6. Joel J. Miller, "Christians Under Attack in Syria, Iran, N. Korea," Patheos, December 7, 2012, http://www.patheos.com/blogs/joeljmiller/2012/12/christians-under-attack-in-syria-iran-n-korea.
7. "Kenya: Pastor Killed in Attack," The Voice of the Martyrs, November 13, 2012, http://www.persecution.com/public/newsroom.aspx?story_ID=NTQ2.

Chapter 10: (Modern) Family Matters

1. Lyndon Azcuna, in discussion with the author, August 2012.
2. Jason DeParle and Sabrina Tavernise, "For Women Under 30, Most Births Occur Outside Marriage," *The New York Times*, February 17, 2012, http://www.nytimes.com/2012/02/18/us/for-women-under-30-most-births-occur-outside-marriage.html?_r=1&pagewanted=all.
3. Herbert S. Klein, "The Changing American Family," *Hoover Digest*, July 30, 2004, http://www.hoover.org/publications/hoover-digest/article/6798.
4. Patrick H. Caddell and Douglas E. Schoen, "Romney, Obama Must Address Crisis of U.S. Families," *Politico*, June 12, 2012,

http://www.politico.com/news/stories/0612/77338_Page2.html#ixzz2347ZLTUC.
5. Andrew Root, "Why Divorce Calls Children's Existence into Question," *Christianity Today*, July 20, 2012, http://www.christianitytoday.com/ct/2012/july-august/why-divorce-calls-childrens-existence-into-question.html?start=3.
6. Ray Pritchard, "What the Bible Says About Homosexuality," sermon preached on October 22, 1989, http://www.keepbelieving.com/sermon/1989-10-22-What-the-Bible-Says-About-Homosexuality.
7. Glenn Stanton, personal correspondence with the author, August 2012.
8. Gary Thomas, in discussion with the author, August 2012.
9. Matthew Lee Anderson, in personal correspondence with the author, August 2012.
10. Denny Burk, "Can Christians Hide in the Basement During the Gay Marriage Debate?" *Denny Burk: A Commentary on Theology, Politics, and Culture* (blog), July 30, 2012, http://www.dennyburk.com/can-christians-hide-in-the-basement-during-the-gay-marriage-debate.
11. Caddell and Schoen.
12. Wayne Grudem, *Politics According to the Bible* (Grand Rapids, MI: Zondervan, 2010), 216.
13. Erin Gieschen, "Rewriting the Fatherless Story," In Touch Ministries, July 2011, http://www.intouch.org/magazine/content/topic/rewriting_the_fatherless_story#.UCP3DDGe5M4.
14. Kristina Rhodes and John Pattison, "Rescuing a Fatherless Generation," *Relevant*, December 3, 2009, http://www.relevantmagazine.com/life/relationship/features/19214-rescuing-a-fatherless-generation.
15. J. D. Greear, "Homosexuality, Christianity, and the Gospel, Part 4," *J. D. Greear: Pastor, Author, Theologian* (blog), April 23, 2012, http://www.jdgreear.com/my_weblog/2012/04/homosexuality-christianity-and-the-gospel-part-4.html.
16. Matthew Lee Anderson.
17. Bill Yaccino, personal correspondence with the author, August 2012.
18. Gary Thomas.
19. Sherri Mueller, in discussion with the author, August 2012.
20. President Barack Obama, quoted in Rhodes and Pattison.

Chapter 11: Beyond Bigger Prisons

1. John W. Whitehead, "Jailing Americans for Profit: The Rise of the Prison Industrial Complex," The Rutherford Institute, April 10, 2012,

https://www.rutherford.org/publications_resources/john_whiteheads_commentary/jailing_americans_for_profit_the_rise_of_the_prison_industrial_complex.

2. Michelle Alexander, *The New Jim Crow: Mass Incarceration in the Age of Colorblindness* (New York: The New Press, 2012), 60.
3. Patrick Egan, "The Declining Culture of Guns and Violence in the United States," *The Monkey Cage* (blog), July 21, 2012, http://themonkeycage.org/blog/2012/07/21/the-declining-culture-of-guns-and-violence-in-the-united-states.
4. Veronique de Rugy, "Prison Math," *Reason*, July 2011, http://reason|.com/archives/2011/06/08/prison-math.
5. Adam Gopnik, "The Caging of America," *The New Yorker*, January 30, 2012, http://www.newyorker.com/arts/critics/atlarge/2012/01/30/120130crat_atlarge_gopnik#ixzz23YV58qmI.
6. Whitehead.
7. Jim Liske, in discussion with the author, August 29, 2012.
8. Liske.
9. Liske.
10. Jim Dailey, "Violence to Peace," *Decision Magazine,* Billy Graham Evangelistic Association, June 1, 2006, http://www.billygraham.org/articlepage.asp?articleid=682.
11. Marvin Olasky, "Work and Faith, Connected," *World*, August 11, 2012, http://www.worldmag.com/articles/19750.
12. From author's personal knowledge and from the bio of Steve Curington, "About the Founder," Reformers Unanimous International Ministries, http://reformu.com/about/what-is-ru/about-the-founder.html.
13. Lyndon Azcuna, in discussion with the author, August 2012.
14. Manny Mill, in discussion with the author, August 2012.
15. Jim Liske, personal correspondence with the author, August 2012.
16. Liske, personal correspondence.
17. Mark Curran, in discussion with the author, August 2012.
18. "More Prison Visits = Less Recidivism," Justice Fellowship, accessed August 14, 2012, http://www.justicefellowship.org/what-is-restorative-justice/justice-fellowship-resources/16168-more-prison-visits-less-recidivism.
19. "Mission Statement," Angel Tree, accessed August 15, 2012, http://www.angeltree.org/why-angel-tree/why-at-second.
20. Manny Mill.
21. Liske, personal correspondence.

Chapter 12: A Theology of Orphans

1. "Mission," Help One Now, accessed December 17, 2012, http://www.helponenow.org/about/helps-story.
2. Chris Marlow, in discussion with the author.
3. "Orphans," Justice and Mercy International, accessed December 17, 2012, http://justiceandmercy.org/initiatives/orphans.
4. David M. Smolin and Elizabeth Bartholet, "The Debate," ed. Judith L. Gibbons and Karen Smith Rotabi, *Intercountry Adoption: Policies, Practices, and Outcomes* (Williston, VT: Ashgate, 2012), accessed December 17, 2012, http://www.law.harvard.edu/faculty/bartholet/The_Debate_1_13_2012.pdf.
5. Bartholet and Smolin.
6. Bartholet and Smolin.
7. Bartholet and Smolin.
8. "Vision," Kidmia, accessed December 17, 2012, http://kidmia.org/vision.
9. John Sowers, *Fatherless Generation: Redeeming the Story* (Grand Rapids, MI: Zondervan, 2010).
10. John Sowers, "90 Teenage Moms at Memphis High School," Fatherless Generation: Redeeming the Story, January 19, 2011, http://fatherlessgeneration.com/thoughts/90-teenage-moms-at-memphis-high-school.

ABOUT THE AUTHORS

DILLON BURROUGHS is an author, activist, and cofounder of Activist Faith. He served in Haiti following the epic 2010 earthquake and has investigated modern slavery in the U.S. and internationally. His more than thirty authored and coauthored books include *Hunger No More*, *Not in My Town* (with Charles Powell), and *Undefending Christianity*. Discover more at DillonBurroughs.org.

DANIEL DARLING is the senior pastor of Gages Lake Bible Church and the author of numerous books, including *iFaith* and *Real*. His work has been featured in *Relevant*, *Christianity Today*, *Focus on the Family*, *OnCourse*, and *The Gospel Coalition*. Daniel holds a bachelor's degree in pastoral ministry from Dayspring Bible College and is pursuing a master's of divinity degree from Trinity Evangelical Divinity School. He and his wife, Angela, have four children and reside in a northern suburb of Chicago.

DAN KING is the founder and president of Fistbump Media LLC, where he helps bloggers, nonprofits, and a variety of other organizations leverage social media tools to tell their stories. He's also the author of *The Unlikely Missionary: From Pew-Warmer to Poverty-Fighter* and several e-books. You can find him coaching and consulting at FistbumpMedia.com and writing about his faith at BibleDude.net. Dan and his wife, Krista, reside with their three (two biological, one adopted) children on the Gulf Coast of Florida.

More from BibleDude Press

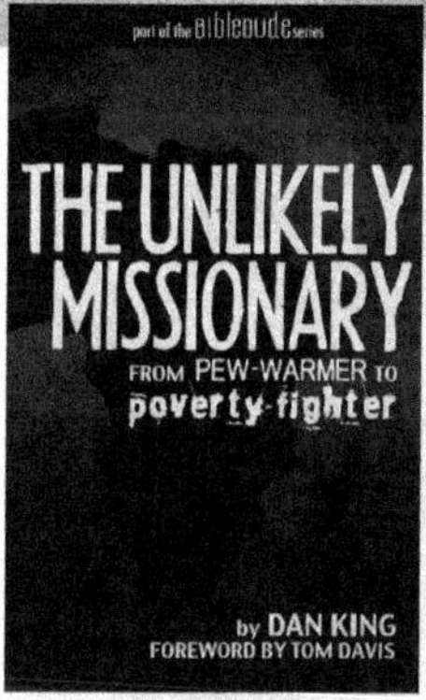

The Unlikely Missionary: From Pew-Warmer to Poverty-Fighter
Dan King

In addition to the stories of people and experiences from a trip to Africa, the book is full of practical ideas and exercises that will challenge you discover world-changing passion whether it takes you half-way around the world or keeps you right at home.

Behold the Beauty: An Invitation to Bible Reading
Monica Sharman

Do you feel unfamiliar with the Bible and want a friendly introduction? Have you been reading the Bible for years but could use a fresh approach—or a flavorful jolt? Are you thinking of inviting a friend to read the Bible, who has never read it before?

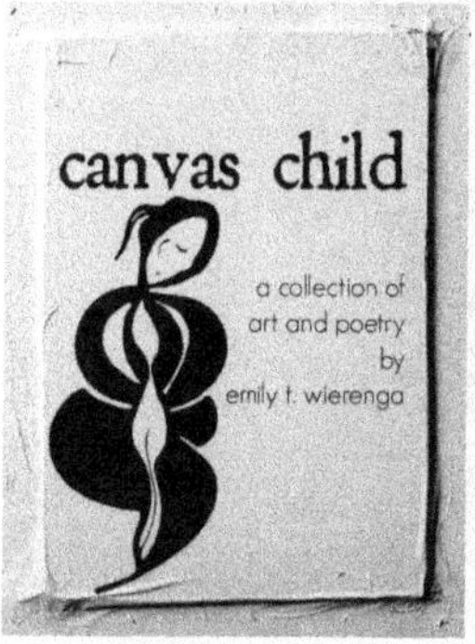

canvas child: a collection of art and poetry
Emily Wierenga

These poems and paintings were created over a period of significant spiritual growth, during which Wierenga was ministering to Young Life kids while battling a relapse into anorexia nervosa. It is her prayer that they will somehow serve to minister to others.

To order copies log on to **www.BibleDude.net**.

BIBLEDUDE PRESS
read pray serve.

www.ingramcontent.com/pod-product-compliance
Lightning Source LLC
LaVergne TN
LVHW052021080426
835513LV00018B/2106
9780692798683